HISTORIANS AT WORK

Does the Frontier Experience Make America Exceptional?

Readings Selected and Introduced by

Richard W. Etulain
University of New Mexico

Selections by

Frederick Jackson Turner

Richard White

Glenda Riley

Martin Ridge

Donald Worster

Patricia Nelson Limerick

Michael P. Malone

Gerald Thompson

Elliott West

Bedford / St. Martin's   *Boston* ◆ *New York*

For Bedford/St. Martin's

History Editor: Katherine E. Kurzman
Developmental Editor: Charisse Kiino
Production Supervisor: Catherine Hetmansky
Marketing Manager: Charles Cavaliere
Editorial Assistant: Molly Kalkstein
Copyeditor: Linda Leet Howe
Text Design: Claire Seng-Niemoeller
Cover Design: Peter Blaiwas
Cover Art: Photograph of Frederick Jackson Turner courtesy of Brown Publishers, Sterling, Pennsylvania
Composition: G&S Typesetters, Inc.
Printing and Binding: Haddon Craftsmen, Inc.

President: Charles H. Christensen
Editorial Director: Joan E. Feinberg
Director of Editing, Design, and Production: Marcia Cohen
Managing Editor: Elizabeth M. Schaaf

Library of Congress Catalog Card Number: 98–83251

Manufactured in the United States of America.

3   2   1   0
f   e   d   c   b

For information, write: Bedford/St. Martin's, 75 Arlington Street, Boston, MA 02116
(617-426-7440)

ISBN: 0–312–18309–7

Acknowledgments

PATRICIA NELSON LIMERICK, "What on Earth Is the New Western History?"; MICHAEL P. MALONE, "The 'New Western History': An Assessment"; GERALD THOMPSON, "Another Look at Frontier versus Western Historiography"; and ELLIOTT WEST, "A Longer, Grimmer, but More Interesting Story," "Why the Past May Be Changing," *Montana: The Magazine of Western History* 40 (Summer 1990), 60–76. Used by permission of *Montana: The Magazine of Western History.*
MARTIN RIDGE, "The Life of an Idea: The Significance of Frederick Jackson Turner's Frontier Thesis," *Montana: The Magazine of Western History* 40 (Winter 1991), 2–13. Used by permission of *Montana: The Magazine of Western History.*
GLENDA RILEY, "Frederick Jackson Turner Overlooked the Ladies." Reprinted by permission from the *Journal of the Early Republic* 13 (Summer 1993), 216–30. Copyright © 1993 by the Society for Historians of the Early American Republic.
RICHARD WHITE, "When Frederick Jackson Turner and Buffalo Bill Cody Both Played Chicago in 1893," from *Frontier and Region: Essays in Honor of Martin Ridge,* pp. 201–12. Used by permission of The University of New Mexico Press.
DONALD WORSTER, "New West, True West: Interpreting the Region's History," *Western Historical Quarterly* 18 (April 1987): 141–56. Copyright by the Western History Association. Reprinted by permission.

Foreword

The short, inexpensive, and tightly focused books in the Historians at Work series set out to show students what historians do by turning closed specialist debate into an open discussion about important and interesting historical problems. These volumes invite students to confront the issues historians grapple with while providing enough support so that students can form their own opinions and join the debate. The books convey the intellectual excitement of "doing history" that should be at the core of any undergraduate study of the discipline. Each volume starts with a contemporary historical question that is posed in the book's title. The question focuses on either an important historical document (the Declaration of Independence, the Emancipation Proclamation) or a major problem or event (the beginnings of American slavery, the Pueblo Revolt of 1680) in American history. An introduction supplies the basic historical context students need and then traces the ongoing debate among historians, showing both how old questions have yielded new answers and how new questions have arisen. Following this two-part introduction are four or five interpretive selections by top scholars, reprinted in their entirety from journals and books, including endnotes. Each selection is either a very recent piece or a classic argument that is still in play and is headed by a question that relates it to the book's core problem. Volumes that focus on a document reprint it in the opening materials so that students can read arguments alongside the evidence and reasoning on which they rest.

One purpose of these books is to show students that they *can* engage with sophisticated writing and arguments. To help them do so, each selection includes apparatus that provides context for engaged reading and critical thinking. An informative headnote introduces the angle of inquiry that the reading explores and closes with Questions for a Closer Reading, which invite students to probe the selection's assumptions, evidence, and argument. At the end of the book, Making Connections questions offer students ways to read the essays against one another, showing how interesting problems emerge from the debate. Suggestions for Further Reading conclude each book, pointing interested students toward relevant materials for extended study.

Historical discourse is rarely a matter of simple opposition. These volumes show how ideas develop and how answers change, as minor themes turn into major considerations. The Historians at Work volumes bring together thoughtful statements in an ongoing conversation about topics that continue to engender debate, drawing students into the historical discussion with enough context and support to participate themselves. These books aim to show how serious scholars have made sense of the past and why what they do is both enjoyable and worthwhile.

EDWARD COUNTRYMAN

Preface

For more than two centuries, Americans and visitors to the United States have dissected our cultural identity. Many of these discussions focus on America as an exceptional or unique society. Seventeenth- and eighteenth-century observers pointed to the isolation from European institutions and the openness of American society as major reasons for its exceptionalism. Other historians and travelers, taking a different tack in the nineteenth century, cited Puritanism, democratic institutions, and even slavery as the primary influences shaping American culture and traditions. In the twentieth century, still other writers stressed abundance, especially in national resources, as the key to understanding America. Since the 1960s, however, hosts of scholars and other students have emphasized multicultural social and ethnic diversities as the most significant factor in defining the United States.

Halfway through these two centuries, in the 1890s, historian Frederick Jackson Turner pinpointed yet another experience as the premier shaping influence of American history and culture. It was the frontier, the westward movement from the Atlantic to the Pacific, Turner asserted, that did more than anything else to define the United States. In 1893, as a young history professor, Turner told a small gathering of historians in Chicago that the frontier made the American past exceptional. By World War I, most historians and many other thoughtful Americans accepted the Turner or frontier thesis as embodied in his essay of 1893, "The Significance of the Frontier in American History." For them, the frontier thesis was the most convincing way to explain the American past and American identity. But in the decades after World War II, scholars and many others increasingly questioned the Turner thesis as an acceptable theory explaining American history and culture. The economic disappointments arising from the Great Depression in the 1930s and the horrors of a global war in the early 1940s made Americans less accepting of as well as more critical of the optimistic frontier doctrine. Despite these criticisms, however, no essay or book about American history attracts as much attention, pro and con, as Turner's essay. It remains a classic piece of American historical writing and worthy of historical debate today.

This collection of essays begins with Turner's thesis and then surveys a range of views from working historians about the frontier thesis and Frederick Jackson Turner. Turner's memorable essay encapsulates the major reasons for considering the frontier as the leading cause of American exceptionalism. But most current writers challenge Turner's interpretation. Richard White, for example, provides a more complex portrait of the frontier, arguing that Turner and Buffalo Bill Cody furnished competing and contrasting perspectives. Glenda Riley points out that Turner's oversight, his nearly total omission of women, severely limits the frontier thesis as an explanation of American exceptionalism.

Martin Ridge and Donald Worster follow other lines of inquiry. The most sympathetic to Turner of the writers presented here, Ridge summarizes the content of the classic frontier essay and discusses the influence of Turner's ideas on subsequent historians. He still finds much to praise in the frontier thesis. Worster, on the other hand, thinks the frontier concept insufficient for explaining the American West. Instead, he urges historians and students to view the West as a separate, evolving region with a unique identity. For Worster, these separate regions, not the frontier, are the keys to understanding American history.

In the final selection, four well-known western historians furnish contending interpretations of the frontier and the American West. Patricia Nelson Limerick defines a New Western history and calls for what she considers a more realistic interpretation of the western past. Although saluting much of what Limerick has to say, Michael P. Malone and Gerald Thompson are less convinced that the New Western history satisfactorily deals with the most significant questions. Finally, Elliott West suggests that the newer, more complex stories being told about the frontier and the American West — perhaps because they are less tied to earlier tales of frontier exceptionalism — add much to our understanding of western history.

Taken together, these essays provide students and other readers a useful sampling of recent thinking and writing about the American frontier and the West and about American exceptionalism. The editorial introduction and the brief headnotes prefacing each essay will also help readers comprehend the general intellectual issues contained in each of the selections. The headnotes also raise questions pertinent to the content and the point of view of the accompanying essay. Finally, the bibliography furnishes commentaries on an abbreviated listing of important books and essays discussing the frontier thesis, Frederick Jackson Turner, and American exceptionalism.

I wish to acknowledge the helpful comments of several readers on an earlier draft of this manuscript. I am grateful for useful reviews from Harry Fritz, University of Montana; Allan G. Bogue, University of Wisconsin, Madison; John Mack Faragher, Yale University; Elliott West, University of Arkansas;

and Glenda Riley, Ball State University. Staff members at Bedford/St. Martin's also provided much direction and encouragement: Chuck Christensen, President; Joan Feinberg, Editorial Director; Katherine Kurzman, Sponsoring Editor; Charisse Kiino, Developmental Editor; and Elizabeth Schaaf, Managing Editor. At the University of New Mexico, I would like to thank David Key and Cindy Tyson for their help in the preparation of the manuscript. To all these colleagues, I am obliged.

RICHARD W. ETULAIN

A Note for Students

Every piece of written history starts when somebody becomes curious and asks questions. The very first problem is who, or what, to study. A historian might ask an old question yet again, after deciding that existing answers are not good enough. But brand-new questions can emerge about old, familiar topics, particularly in light of new findings or directions in research, such as the rise of women's history in the late 1970s.

In one sense history is all that happened in the past. In another it is the universe of potential evidence that the past has bequeathed. But written history does not exist until a historian collects and probes that evidence (*research*), makes sense of it (*interpretation*), and shows to others what he or she has seen so that they can see it too (*writing*). Good history begins with respecting people's complexity, not with any kind of preordained certainty. It might well mean using modern techniques that were unknown at the time, such as Freudian psychology or statistical assessment by computer. But good historians always approach the past on its own terms, taking careful stock of the period's cultural norms and people's assumptions or expectations, no matter how different from contemporary attitudes. Even a few decades can offer a surprisingly large gap to bridge, as each generation discovers when it evaluates the accomplishments of those who have come before.

To write history well requires three qualities. One is the courage to try to understand people whom we never can meet — unless our subject is very recent — and to explain events that no one can re-create. The second quality is the humility to realize that we can never entirely appreciate either the people or the events under study. However much evidence is compiled and however smart the questions posed, the past remains too large to contain. It will always continue to surprise.

The third quality historians need is the curiosity that turns sterile facts into clues about a world that once was just as alive, passionate, frightening, and exciting as our own, yet in different ways. Today we know how past events "turned out." But the people taking part had no such knowledge. Good history recaptures those people's fears, hopes, frustrations, failures, and achievements; it tells about people who faced the predicaments and choices that still confront us as we head into the twenty-first century.

All the essays collected in this volume bear on a single, shared problem that the authors agree is important, however differently they may choose to respond to it. On its own, each essay reveals a fine mind coming to grips with a worthwhile question. Taken together, the essays give a sense of just how complex the human situation can be. That point — that human situations are complex — applies just as much to life today as to the lives led in the past. History has no absolute "lessons" to teach; it follows no invariable "laws." But knowing about another time might be of some help as we struggle to live within our own.

EDWARD COUNTRYMAN

Contents

PART ONE

Introduction

*The Frontier and
American Exceptionalism*

The Frontier and
American Exceptionalism

Frederick Jackson Turner and the Frontier

I was speaking to a large student gathering in the Philippine Islands when a young woman from the audience raised her hand and asked a forthright question: "Why do you Americans think you're so successful?" Although her query carried a tone of accusation, it also raised an important question that has perplexed Americans and foreign observers since at least the late eighteenth century: If the United States has spawned an exceptional society and culture, what forces have shaped that distinctive identity?

As early as the American Revolution, questions about American exceptionalism surfaced. Had a New World society and culture emerged different from those in western Europe? If so, what was unique about this new America, and how had this new society gradually evolved? In this vein, the French-American Hector St. John de Crèvecoeur asked in his *Letters from an American Farmer* (1782), "What then is the American, this new man?" Answering his own question, Crèvecoeur asserted that the American was a new breed, a composite but independent and individualistic pioneer. A half-century later, the French traveler Alexis de Tocqueville pointed to the equality of classes as the root of America's exceptionalism. Other nineteenth-century observers singled out Puritanism, democratic institutions, or the slave and plantation society as its most distinguishing features.[1]

All these views gained adherents during the nineteenth century, but the most widely circulated statement of American exceptionalism was pronounced in July 1893 in Chicago. Frederick Jackson Turner, a thirty-one-year-old history professor at the University of Wisconsin, appeared before the annual meeting of the American Historical Association to deliver a paper, "The Significance of the Frontier in American History." On that hot and humid July evening at the Columbian Exposition taking place on the famed White City grounds in Chicago, the young historian presented what became the most significant essay about American history. It was a provocative call to understand American identity as primarily the result of the shifting national frontiers, advancing from the Atlantic to the Pacific Coast.[2]

At the time, neither the audience attending Turner's lecture nor other historians seemed greatly taken with Turner's ideas. Although journalists, historians, and other scholars mentioned the paper, they did so only in passing. But within a decade, by the early 1900s, the Turner or "frontier thesis" began to dominate new thinking and writing about American history, especially works on the American frontier and the West. By 1910, when Turner became president of the American Historical Association and accepted appointment to a chair at Harvard, he was at the top of his profession, his ideas exerting a clear influence on most American historians. Although few might have thought so in 1893, Turner's thesis helped reorient American historical writing, providing a new way to define American identity and laying out a fresh method by which to interpret the frontier and the American West.

In his essay as in other writings of the 1890s, Turner revealed a great deal about his own background and intellectual maturation. His profound interest in the frontier arose naturally. Born on November 14, 1861, in Portage, Wisconsin, a frontier town of nearly four thousand, Turner grew up in a community awash in the fresh memories of exploration and settlement. As Turner's biographer wrote, Portage was a town "bursting with optimism and cockily confident of the future."[3] After graduating from public high school in Portage, where he compiled an outstanding record for scholastic achievement, exemplary deportment, and noteworthy oratory, Turner entered the University of Wisconsin, Madison, in the fall of 1878.

Turner soon became a history major. Under the skilled teaching of William F. Allen, a winsome and vivacious professor, Turner quickly made great strides, first as an undergraduate and then as a graduate student in history. So impressive was his record, he was hired as an assistant in the Wisconsin history department. Encouraged to pursue a doctorate, Turner enrolled in the Ph.D. program at Johns Hopkins University in Baltimore. There he fell under the influence of Herbert Baxter Adams and other scholars who preached the "germ" doctrine, which emphasized the direct, persisting influence of European institutions on New World society and culture. Turner completed his doctorate in 1891 with a dissertation on the Indian fur trade in Wisconsin, a work that emphasized not so much the shaping power of the frontier as the Old World impact on wilderness institutions.[4]

Turner, now married and soon to be a father, had returned to Madison in 1889 before finishing his Ph.D. to resume his position in the history department. He quickly gained a reputation as an inspiring teacher, helpful colleague, and provocative thinker and in the 1890s turned out a clutch of important essays, although he failed to complete any of his promised books. After the publication of his frontier essay in 1894 and following his participation in professional meetings over the next few years, he began to receive offers from other universities, which he used to bargain for a lighter teaching load and additional research time at the Wisconsin campus.

The events of 1910 dramatically changed the direction of Turner's career. As the president of the American Historical Association and the holder of a prestigious chair in history at Harvard, he had reached the twin peaks in any American historian's career. But these achievements carried unexpected costs. Called upon to make numerous public presentations in the Harvard academic community, loaded down with other energy-draining assignments, and isolated from many of his frontier sources, Turner wobbled, unable to finish his book-length projects. Although these wider professional worlds enlarged Turner's reputation, they also ate up his time and undermined his health. In fact, Turner failed to complete any new books before his death in 1932. In addition, even though his collection of previously published essays, *The Frontier in American History* (1920), received positive reviews, Turner turned increasingly to the study of the West as a separate, identifiable region.[5]

Turner retired from Harvard in 1924 and eventually moved to southern California, where he worked diligently at the Huntington Library. But declining health, his proclivity for researching several topics simultaneously, and his flagging energies forestalled the completion of his books. After his death, some of his essays on regionalism were published as *The Significance of Sections in American History* (1932), which won a Pulitzer Prize. A huge, unfinished volume of his work, edited and polished by his devoted secretary and other scholars, appeared posthumously as *The United States, 1830–1850: The Nation and Its Sections* (1935).[6] Even though Turner's last writing dealt with evolving regions rather than with new frontiers, it still evidenced his large, lifetime interest in exploring how the frontier shaped American history and culture. On the frontier, "antagonism to the restraints of government" reinforced the democracy, self-reliance, individualism, and capitalism he saw nearly omnipresent beyond the Appalachians.[7] To the end, Turner remained convinced, as he had been nearly forty years earlier, that the frontier was the most powerful molding force in the American past.

Turner's definition of "frontier" needs further elaboration. For him, the frontier experience meant the physical movement of European settlers across the American continent. Because of his own background and his attachment to agricultural communities, farmers were the central figures of his frontier story. True, explorers, fur trappers, railroad builders, stockraisers, and townsmen were part of the westward movement traced from East to West, but the hard-working farmers were the major protagonists of his histories. For Turner, an understanding of American exceptionalism demanded an understanding of the experiences of farmers on the westward-moving frontier.

When the 1890 census declared the frontier closed because the mushrooming population had settled previously open areas, Frederick Jackson Turner was moved to define the impact of that centuries-old frontier on American history. With his contemporaries he pointed to the evidence: Most significantly, Native Americans were now settled on reservations, railroads crisscrossed much of the country west of the Mississippi, and in his view, nearly all the farmable land had been claimed, as cities, towns, and hamlets dotted the West. Schools, churches, and other institutions were irrefutable proof that civilization and culture had arrived and settled the frontier.

When Turner returned to Madison from Johns Hopkins in 1889, he still seemed captive to the "germ theory" school, which emphasized the shaping power of European institutions in the New World. His emphasis soon changed and became clearer in two notable essays Turner published on the meaning of history, the importance of the frontier, and American exceptionalism. In the earlier of the two, "The Significance of History" (1891), Turner provided a stimulating credo for instructors and students of history. They had to learn, he said, that *"each age writes the history of the past anew with reference to the conditions uppermost in its own time."*[8] It was Turner's life-long conviction that historians must emphasize the important, pragmatic links between the past and the present, the local and the global. But he also issued a strong warning that present-day historians often overlook. He cautioned his listeners that they must write with "historical imagination and sympathy that does not judge the past by canons of the present, nor read into it the ideas of the present" (55).

The following year, in "Problems in American History" (1892), Turner spoke more explicitly about the significance of the frontier and American exceptionalism. Like a performer delivering a series of power points, Turner told readers of the university's undergraduate newspaper, *The Aegis,* how they ought to rethink American history.[9] Instead of focusing on European precedents, they needed to realize that "the fundamental, dominating fact in United States history" was the shore to shore expansion of settlement. "In a sense, American history up to our own day," he wrote, "has been colonial history, the colonization of the Great West. This ever retreating frontier of free land is the key to American development" (72). Turner also revealed his interest in the relationship between people and land by asserting that close scrutiny of the receding American frontier would reveal how free land, "physiographic" [geographical] sections, and the presence of Native Americans determined the course of American history.

Lest his readers overlook his major point, Turner told them again that "the real lines of American development, the forces dominating our character, are to be studied in the history of westward expansion" (72). What made the United States exceptional was its frontier experience, not European legacies at work in the New World. Then, as he often did, Turner closed with one of his memorable rhetorical flourishes: "What the Mediterranean Sea was to the Greeks, breaking the bond of custom, offering new experiences, calling out new institutions and activities, that the ever retreating Great West has been to the eastern United States directly, and to the nations of Europe more remotely" (83).

Clearly Turner had announced his original ideas before 1893, but in that often-cited frontier thesis essay he preached a sermon heard around American historiographical circles throughout the next century. It not only pointed to the limitations of previous interpretations, it also laid out, in abbreviated form, the storyline for a new way of narrating American history. Capitalizing on the keen desire of a historical profession and a general public for a nationalistic, even chauvinistic, portrayal of its exceptional past, Turner fashioned an interpretation of American history that converted specialists and laypeople alike.

In his frontier essay delivered in 1893 and initially printed the next year, Turner told his fellow historians, first of all, that they had to shift their focus.[10] Previous historians had overemphasized slavery and other constitutional issues. Others were too tied to the study of European "germs" or origins. Like a good drill sergeant, Turner told his troops to do an about-face: They should turn away from Europe toward a westward-moving frontier. There lay the meaning of the country's unique experience. In one terse sentence early in his essay, Turner encapsulated his major themes: "The existence of an area of free land, its continuous recession, and the advance of American settlement westward, explain American development" (199). If Americans wanted to understand the significance of their past, Turner, like many of his contemporaries, offered a patriotic explanation: the settling of the New World, especially the American frontier, was the most powerful force in shaping exceptional Americans. A century later, many interpreters consider these buoyant pronouncements evidence of Turner's excessive triumphalism. But Turner and his contemporaries took up the frontier doctrine as if it issued new marching orders for the advance of international Americanism.[11]

Attempting to show that Americans had incorporated their experiences into new principles of action and thought, Turner traced earlier frontier contacts with new lands and Indians through a series of evolutionary stages that ultimately produced particular "intellectual traits" that emerged from these stages of frontier activity. As a committed social and cultural evolutionist, the Wisconsin historian studied the accretions of western experiences that had, over time, been laminated into a composite American character. Turner pointed to several important factors that he saw arising from unique frontier experiences: a "composite nationality," which others would later call a melting pot; the "growth of democracy"; an independent individualism; and economic and physical mobility. "The result," Turner concluded, was "that to the frontier the American intellect [owed] its striking characteristics" (226–27).

But Turner was not satisfied to list, analyze, and evaluate. Wanting his listeners and readers to engage emotionally with these descriptions and hold on to these tradition-molding truths, he concluded with two powerful and grandiloquent phrases. The first repeated the orotund ending of the previous year's essay comparing the custom-shattering influences of the Mediterranean Sea on the Greeks and of the frontier on Americans. The second pinpointed the watershed importance of the frontier: "And now, four centuries from the discovery of America, at the end of a hundred years of life under the Constitution, the frontier has gone, and with its going has closed the first period of American history" (227). These lines, which vividly illustrate Turner's frequent juxtaposition of rhetorical flourish and interpretation, were the emotional high point of his early career.

Less well known but equally significant was Turner's criticism of contemporary interpretations of the frontier West. As he told a correspondent three decades later, other writers in the 1880s and early 1890s had been too caught up in depicting the frontier as a "Wild West." Rather than analyze the significance of notable frontier institutions, they had chronicled the lively events and heroic demigods of a frenetic landscape. Turner endeavored to lead interpreters of the West in a more analytical, less romantic direction.[12]

Turner clearly distinguished between his views and those of Wild West romanticists when he stated that "much has been written about the frontier from the view of border warfare and the chase, but as a field for the serious study of the economist and the historian it has been neglected" (200). For Turner, historians like Francis Parkman and his own contemporaries Theodore Roosevelt, Justin Winsor, and Reuben Gold Thwaites too often stressed adventure or failed to adopt an interpretive approach to the past. He tried to steer his readers away from such misguided notions about the western past.[13]

Turner saved his sharpest darts for those he considered the greater sinners. A key but often overlooked footnote in his frontier essay conveys his disgust for sensational accounts of a Wild West: "I have refrained from dwelling on the lawless characteristics of the frontier," he writes, "because they are sufficiently well known. The gambler and desperado, the regulators of the Carolinas and the vigilantes of California, are types of that line of scum that the waves of advancing civilization bore before them, and of the growth of spontaneous organs of authority where legal authority was absent" (223). Who was it that spun out this "line of scum" Turner so detested? Turner probably referred to the Local Color writers and dime novelists whose portrayals of the West stretched well beyond the facts. The western Local Color stories—by Bret Harte and Alfred Henry Lewis, two widely read writers, and Joaquin Miller, a poet—celebrated gamblers, desperadoes, prostitutes, and romantic explorers and cowboys. Even more sensational were the thousands of dime novels turned out by easterners eager to dramatize a West of scouts, "savages," renegades, and cowboys. By 1890, even a good deal of historical writing about the West treated readers to this steady diet of outlandish adventure stories, far removed from the historical reality Frederick Jackson Turner sought to describe.[14]

Most of all, Turner attempted to counter the enormous influence of "Buffalo Bill" Cody's Wild West extravaganza. Launched in 1883, Cody's arena show swept to international popularity over the next decade. If Turner called for an analytical, interpretive history of the frontier, Buffalo Bill carefully blended competition, conflict, and violence into a dramatic narrative of a romantic West.[15] In fact, the same day in July 1893 that Turner presented his frontier thesis at the Chicago World's Fair, just five miles away Buffalo Bill paraded his performers before an audience of several thousand enthusiastic spectators. Although some recent interpreters link Turner to these late nineteenth-century dramatizations of an untamed Wild West, throughout his early career he roundly criticized such exaggerated accounts, encouraging instead careful studies of the frontier's significance.[16] Just as Turner challenged earlier slavery-driven and European "germ" interpretations of American history, he sidelined Wild West versions to clear the way for his own more explanatory approach.

Historians and the Turner Thesis

Frederick Jackson Turner occupies a unique position in American historical writing. Beginning his professional career in about 1890, Turner undertook a revision of existing interpretations of the American past, did so successfully, and lived to see his own alternative interpretation of the frontier become the accepted view. No other American historian achieved as much. One hundred years later, near the beginning of another new century, although few American historians would call themselves Turnerians, his thesis remains the most widely discussed interpretation of the American past. In the century since Turner presented his thesis in Chicago, however, it has traversed a series of interpretive peaks and valleys.

Before the Great Depression of the 1930s, few historians found major fault with the frontier thesis. One or two reviewers might have quibbled over Turner's soaring syntax and inexact diction when he advanced his sweeping overview, and others called for more empirical evidence before swallowing Turner's agenda whole. The most substantive reservations came from the distinguished American historian Charles Beard, who argued that Turner paid too much attention to the frontier and underestimated the molding power of economic forces such as slavery and the plantation system, industrialization, and worker-owner conflicts.[17] But these reservations were exceptions. More typical were the effusive reactions of Frederic Logan Paxson, Turner's successor at the University of Wisconsin and perhaps the country's best-known frontier specialist after Turner. Turner died in March 1932, and later that year, Paxson prepared the first historiographical overview of the frontier thesis, "A Generation of the Frontier Hypothesis: 1893–1932." Paxson confirmed its staying power, but then in a notable twist, added, "We can account for the weakness of the straggling attack upon his hypothesis by the inherent weakness of the case against it."[18]

During the next three decades, commentators raised further reservations about Turner's thesis. During the depths of the depression, many wondered whether it and other exceptionalist themes could stand if the United States proved so helpless against the economic onslaught sweeping through other countries and societies around the world. Moreover, when the Yale historian George Wilson Pierson surveyed the profession in 1941, he discovered that many found much in Turner to quarrel about. The frontier thesis, they argued, was based on an outdated social evolutionist framework. They were also convinced that Turner was blind to many "continuities in the lives of the pioneers and their institutions" and overlooked "much of the seamy side of frontiering."[19] Despite this mounting criticism, Ray Allen Billington's monumental overview, *Westward Expansion: A History of the American Frontier* (1949), which embraced many of Turner's ideas as well as his narrative framework, garnered numerous positive reviews and became the most widely adopted western history text during the next two decades.

Meanwhile, two other interpretations of the frontier and the American West began to gain attention. Herbert Eugene Bolton, one of Turner's former students, urged scholars and students to pay much more heed to what he called the "Spanish Borderlands" and the "Epic of Greater America." Bolton wanted more scrutiny of the varied frontiers of the Western Hemisphere, particularly of the composite cultures along the southern border of the United States. In the early 1930s, Walter Prescott Webb, a Texan, provided another view in his remarkable book, *The Great Plains* (1931). Webb called attention to the significant power of the flat, arid, and treeless plains, environmental themes that gained tremendous popularity after the 1960s. Bolton and Webb were not critics of Turner and his frontier thesis as much as they were advocates of alternative interpretations of the frontier. They were also suggesting that the frontier was not the only possible source of American exceptionalism.

These competing interpretations were light jabs compared to the knock-out blows, beginning in the 1970s, that other historians increasingly rained on Turner and the frontier thesis. Revisionists (those who contradict or revise previous views) of all stripes pointed to many inadequacies in previous writings about the frontier and the American West. So numerous were these attacks that by the 1990s some observers mistakenly declared the frontier thesis essentially dead.[20] As the essays by Martin Ridge and Gerald Thomson reprinted here indicate, however, more than a few historians still found much that was acceptable in Turner's ideas.

The criticism was of several kinds. Some historians emphasized what they considered the weaknesses of the frontier school in acknowledging the large contributions of racial and ethnic minorities to the history of the frontier and the West. Others, as Glenda Riley's essay illustrates, criticized the Turnerians for overlooking the contributions of women to western history. No less pointed were the attacks launched against frontier historians for failing to deal with important questions of gender and class. Some critics also harpooned western specialists for ignoring the post-1900 West and significant urban and environmental subjects. Although most did not explicitly address the subject of exceptionalism, they implied that a perspective as shaky as they now considered the frontier thesis could not be the basis for a tenable interpretation of American culture.

In the late 1980s and 1990s criticism of Turner and frontier interpretations of American history mounted. In 1987 Patricia Nelson Limerick's remarkable book, *The Legacy of Conquest,* was published, and four years later, Richard White's mammoth text, *"It's Your Misfortune and None of My Own,"* appeared. In between, in September 1989, a notable conference entitled "Trails: Toward a New Western History" convened in Santa Fe. A few weeks before this conference, the editor of this volume asked Professor Limerick for a definition of the New Western history. She provided a one-page manifesto that has been widely cited as a succinct summary of the new movement.[21]

New Western historians, according to Limerick, were dissatisfied with previous interpretations of the frontier and the American West. They also wanted to furnish a new, more useful way of studying these subjects. From the outset, they found little that was acceptable in Turner's ideas about the frontier or American exceptionalism; instead, they called for a study of the West as an evolving region and for research on the complexities of race, ethnicity, and gender. Turner had provided an excessively triumphant story; now, however, we needed a more realistic view that did not shy away from the racism, environmental degradation, and economic selfishness of the past. Although the most prominent of the New Western historians — Limerick, Richard White, and Donald Worster, all of whose essays are reprinted here — do not agree on every point, they accept little of the frontier and exceptionalist doctrine Turner preached so passionately.

In light of this powerful criticism, a few questions need to be asked. Is Frederick Jackson Turner dead or alive? Or, phrased differently, has Turner's influence so waned that his ideas lack any suasive power in interpreting American history and culture at the beginning of the twenty-first century? Conversely, despite the limitations of Turner's doctrine, can we argue that his ideas still shape the way we tell American historical stories? Can we yet benefit from Turner's thesis as we narrate American history from the earliest inhabitants to the near present? Any serious student of American history must consider these important issues.

As students read Turner's classic 1893 essay and those by leading historians of the past generation reacting to Turner's frontier and exceptionalist ideas, they should ponder carefully our shifting interpretations of the past. If we now realize that Turner illustrated the nationalistic and exclusionist tendencies of his contemporaries, what are the limitations of our own views? Do our experiences and prejudices also limit and skew our visions of Turner and the past? Should we be as doubtful of our own conclusions about the frontier and American history as we are about the Turner thesis and the convictions of American exceptionalism? This collection of essays should help students and instructors alike to examine and evaluate the important relationships between past and present and how these linkages continue to influence our interpretations of American history.

Notes

1. This introduction draws on the discussion of Frederick Jackson Turner and the frontier thesis in Richard W. Etulain, *Re-imagining the Modern American West: A Century of Fiction, History, and Art* (Tucson: University of Arizona Press, 1996).

2. The three most useful biographical sources on Turner are Ray Allen Billington, *Frederick Jackson Turner: Historian, Scholar, Teacher* (New York: Oxford University Press, 1973); Wilbur R. Jacobs, *On Turner's Trail: 100 Years of Writing Western History* (Lawrence: University Press of Kansas, 1994); and Allan G. Bogue, *Frederick Jackson Turner: Strange Roads Going Down* (Norman: University of Oklahoma Press, 1998).

3. Billington, *Frederick Jackson Turner*, 6.

4. Ray Allen Billington, *The Genesis of the Frontier Thesis: A Study in Historical Creativity* (San Marino, Calif.: Huntington Library, 1971), 15, 239.

5. Frederick Jackson Turner, *The Frontier in American History* (New York: Holt, 1920).

6. Turner, *The Significance of Sections in American History* (New York: Holt, 1932); Turner, *The United States, 1830–1850: The Nation and Its Sections* (New York: Holt, 1935).

7. Turner, *The United States, 1830–1850*, 20.

8. Turner, "The Significance of History," *Wisconsin Journal of Education* 21 (October–November 1891): 230–34, 253–56; reprinted in *The Early Writings of Frederick Jackson Turner* (Madison: University of Wisconsin, 1938), 43–68, quote on p. 52. After initial full citations, this and other Turner essays will be cited by page number in the text. Turner's "Significance of History" receives probing treatment in William Cronon, "Turner's First Stand: The Significance of Significance in American History," in *Writing Western History: Essays on Major Western Historians*, ed. Richard W. Etulain (Albuquerque: University of New Mexico Press, 1991), 73–101. John Mack Faragher brings together ten of Turner's most important essays and adds very useful commentary in his *Rereading Frederick Jackson Turner* (New York: Holt, 1994).

9. "Problems in American History," *Aegis* 7 (November 4, 1892): 48–52; reprinted in *Early Writings*, 71–83.

10. Turner's classic essay appeared first as Frederick J. Turner, "The Significance of the Frontier in American History," in the *Annual Report of the American Historical Association for the Year 1893* (Washington, D.C.: GPO and American Historical Association, 1894), 199–227.

11. For useful criticism of Turner, see the essays collected in this volume. The fullest listings of Turner's writings and comments about him and his ideas are contained in Vernon E. Mattson and William E. Marion, *Frederick Jackson Turner: A Reference Guide* (Boston: G. K. Hall, 1985). Also helpful is Gerald D. Nash, *Creating the West: Historical Interpretations, 1890–1990* (Albuquerque: University of New Mexico Press, 1991); the essays gathered in Patricia Nelson Limerick, Clyde A. Milner II, and Charles E. Rankin, eds., *Trails: Toward a New Western History* (Lawrence: University Press of Kansas, 1991); and Gene M. Gressley, ed., *Old West/New West: Quo Vadis?* (1994; Norman: University of Oklahoma Press, 1997).

12. See Turner's letter to Constance Skinner, March 15, 1922, Turner Papers, box 31, Henry E. Huntington Library, San Marino, California.

13. Differences between Turner's views and Wild West interpretations are discussed in Etulain, *Re-imagining the Modern American West.*

14. Especially useful discussions of late-nineteenth century western American literature are available in J. Golden Taylor and Thomas J. Lyon et al., eds., *A Literary History of the American West* (Fort Worth: Texas Christian University Press, 1987).

15. For an interpretation that differs from the discussion here of Turner and Buffalo Bill Cody, see Richard White, "Frederick Jackson Turner and Buffalo Bill," in *The Frontier in American Culture*, ed. James R. Grossman (Berkeley: University of California Press, 1994), 6–65; and White, "When Frederick Jackson Turner and Buffalo Bill Both Played Chicago in 1893," in *Frontier and Region: Essays in Honor of Martin Ridge*, ed. Robert C. Ritchie and Paul Andrew Hutton (Albuquerque: University of New Mexico Press, 1997), 201–12. White's article appears on pp. 46–57 in this book.

16. The American Studies scholar Richard Slotkin compares the three frontiers of Theodore Roosevelt, Buffalo Bill, and Turner in his book *Gunfighter Nation: The Myth of the Frontier in Twentieth-Century America* (New York: Atheneum, 1992).

17. Charles A. Beard, "The Frontier in American History," *New Republic* 25 (February 16, 1921): 349–50. In addition to the sources listed in n. 11, also see the

helpful comments in David M. Wrobel, *The End of American Exceptionalism: Frontier Anxiety from the Old West to the New Deal* (Lawrence: University Press of Kansas, 1993).

18. Frederic Logan Paxson, "A Generation of the Frontier Hypothesis: 1893–1932," *Pacific Historical Review* 2 (March 1933): 51.

19. Here I am following the probing overview of interpretations of Turner in Allan G. Bogue, "The Course of Western History's First Century," in *A New Significance: Re-envisioning the History of the American West,* ed. Clyde A. Milner II (New York: Oxford University Press, 1996), 3–28, quotes on p. 12. See also George W. Pierson, "American Historians and the Frontier Hypothesis in 1941," parts 1 and 2, *Wisconsin Magazine of History* 26 (September 1942): 36–60; (December 1942): 170–85.

20. For a brief discussion of western historiography, consult Charles S. Peterson, "Speaking for the Past," in *The Oxford History of the American West,* ed. Clyde A. Milner II et al. (New York: Oxford University Press, 1994), 743–69. See also the collected essays in Etulain, ed., *Writing Western History: Essays on Major Western Historians.*

21. The manifesto is contained in Patricia Nelson Limerick, "What on Earth Is the New Western History?" *Montana: The Magazine of Western History* 40 (Summer 1990): 61–64. Limerick's essay appears on pp. 108–13 in this book.

PART TWO

Some Current Questions

The selections that follow deal with some of the issues
about the frontier and American exceptionalism that
now interest historians. Other questions and other
selections could have been chosen, but these show
the current state of the conversation. Each selection
is preceded by a headnote that introduces both its
specific subject and its author. After the headnote
come Questions for a Closer Reading. The headnote
and the questions offer signposts that will allow you
to understand more readily what the author is saying.
The selections are uncut and they include the original
notes. The notes are also signposts for further exploration. If an issue that the author raises intrigues you,
use the notes to follow it up. At the end of all the selections are more questions, under the heading Making Connections. Turn to these after you have read
the selections, and use them to bring the whole discussion together. In order to answer them, you may find
that you need to reread. But no historical source yields
up all that is within it to a person content to read it
just once.

1. How was the idea of the "frontier" born?

Frederick Jackson Turner

The Significance of the Frontier in American History

Although other historians and authors wrote about the importance of the frontier in American history before Frederick Jackson Turner, his classic essay of 1893 did more than any other work to bring the subject to the attention of scholars and general readers. By 1920 the frontier or Turner thesis had become the most widely accepted interpretation of American history.

In his essay Turner made several important points. Now that the census of 1890 has declared the frontier closed, Turner wrote, we need to examine the importance of the frontier experience to American history. After urging his listeners and readers to avoid overemphasizing other subjects, Turner argued that the frontier was *the* most important shaping force in American history. What made Americans unique and exceptional, he said, was the frontier's clear impact on the nation's past. American democracy, nationalism, individualism, and physical and social mobility could be directly linked to the frontier.

In advancing these views, Turner spoke for many of his contemporaries. Convinced that their history and heritage represented useful models of thinking and achievement for other cultures, Americans came to accept Turner's explanation of these unique experiences. It was a nationalistic, patriotic perspective that echoed the attitude of many Americans at the beginning of the twentieth century.

Questions for a Closer Reading

1. How does Turner define "frontier"?

2. According to Turner, what are the most important influences of the frontier on American history?

3. Which of these influences does Turner make the strongest case for and why?

4. What did Turner say about Indians? What role did they play in his frontier drama?

5. Critics of Turner say he underemphasized the complexity of the frontier experience and overemphasized the role of white men. Do you agree? Why or why not?

6. In what specific ways did Turner think the frontier cultivated democracy and individualism? Do you agree or disagree?

7. How do you react to Turner's argument that the frontier was the single most important experience in shaping American history?

The Significance of the Frontier in American History [1]

In a recent bulletin of the Superintendent of the Census for 1890 appear these significant words: "Up to and including 1880 the country had a frontier of settlement, but at present the unsettled area has been so broken into by isolated bodies of settlement that there can hardly be said to be a frontier line. In the discussion of its extent, its westward movement, etc., it can not, therefore, any longer have a place in the census reports." This brief official statement marks the closing of a great historic movement. Up to our own day American history has been in a large degree the history

---

Frederick Jackson Turner, "The Significance of the Frontier in American History," *Annual Report of the American Historical Association for the Year 1893* (Washington, D.C.: GPO and American Historical Association, 1894), 199–227.

of the colonization of the Great West. The existence of an area of free land, its continuous recession, and the advance of American settlement westward, explain American development.

Behind institutions, behind constitutional forms and modifications, lie the vital forces that call these organs into life and shape them to meet changing conditions. The peculiarity of American institutions is, the fact that they have been compelled to adapt themselves to the changes of an expanding people — to the changes involved in crossing a continent, in winning a wilderness, and in developing at each area of this progress out of the primitive economic and political conditions of the frontier into the complexity of city life. Said Calhoun in 1817, "We are great, and rapidly — I was about to say fearfully — growing!"[2] So saying, he touched the distinguishing feature of American life. All peoples show development; the germ theory of politics has been sufficiently emphasized. In the case of most nations, however, the development has occurred in a limited area; and if the nation has expanded, it has met other growing peoples whom it has conquered. But in the case of the United States we have a different phenomenon. Limiting our attention to the Atlantic coast, we have the familiar phenomenon of the evolution of institutions in a limited area, such as the rise of representative government; the differentiation of simple colonial governments into complex organs; the progress from primitive industrial society, without division of labor, up to manufacturing civilization. But we have in addition to this a recurrence of the process of evolution in each western area reached in the process of expansion. Thus American development has exhibited not merely advance along a single line, but a return to primitive conditions on a continually advancing frontier line, and a new development for that area. American social development has been continually beginning over again on the frontier. This perennial rebirth, this fluidity of American life, this expansion westward with its new opportunities, its continuous touch with the simplicity of primitive society, furnish the forces dominating American character. The true point of view in the history of this nation is not the Atlantic coast, it is the great West. Even the slavery struggle, which is made so exclusive an object of attention by writers like Prof. von Holst, occupies its important place in American history because of its relation to westward expansion.

In this advance, the frontier is the outer edge of the wave — the meeting point between savagery and civilization. Much has been written about the frontier from the point of view of border warfare and the chase, but as a field for the serious study of the economist and the historian it has been neglected.

The American frontier is sharply distinguished from the European frontier — a fortified boundary line running through dense populations. The most significant thing about the American frontier is, that it lies at the hither edge of free land. In the census reports it is treated as the margin of that settlement which has a density of two or more to the square mile. The term is an elastic one, and for our purposes does not need sharp definition. We shall consider the whole frontier belt, including the Indian country and the outer margin of the "settled area" of the census reports. This paper will make no attempt to treat the subject exhaustively; its aim is simply to call attention to the frontier as a fertile field for investigation, and to suggest some of the problems which arise in connection with it.

In the settlement of America we have to observe how European life entered the continent, and how America modified and developed that life and reacted on Europe. Our early history is the study of European germs developing in an American environment. Too exclusive attention has been paid by institutional students to the Germanic origins, too little to the American factors. The frontier is the line of most rapid and effective Americanization. The wilderness masters the colonist. It finds him a European in dress, industries, tools, modes of travel, and thought. It takes him from the railroad car and puts him in the birch canoe. It strips off the garments of civilization and arrays him in the hunting shirt and the moccasin. It puts him in the log cabin of the Cherokee and Iroquois and runs an Indian palisade around him. Before long he has gone to planting Indian corn and plowing with a sharp stick; he shouts the war cry and takes the scalp in orthodox Indian fashion. In short, at the frontier the environment is at first too strong for the man. He must accept the conditions which it furnishes, or perish, and so he fits himself into the Indian clearings and follows the Indian trails. Little by little he transforms the wilderness, but the outcome is not the old Europe, not simply the development of Germanic germs, any more than the first phenomenon was a case of reversion to the Germanic mark. The fact is, that here is a new product that is American. At first, the frontier was the Atlantic coast. It was the frontier of Europe in a very real sense. Moving westward, the frontier became more and more American. As successive terminal moraines result from successive glaciations, so each frontier leaves its traces behind it, and when it becomes a settled area the region still partakes of the frontier characteristics. Thus the advance of the frontier has meant a steady movement away from the influence of Europe, a steady growth of independence on American lines. And to study this advance, the men who grew up under these conditions, and the political, economic, and social results of it, is to study the really American part of our history.

Stages of Frontier Advance

In the course of the seventeenth century the frontier was advanced up the Atlantic river courses, just beyond the "fall line," and the tidewater region became the settled area. In the first half of the eighteenth century another advance occurred. Traders followed the Delaware and Shawnese Indians to the Ohio as early as the end of the first quarter of the century.[3] Gov. Spotswood, of Virginia, made an expedition in 1714 across the Blue Ridge. The end of the first quarter of the century saw the advance of the Scotch-Irish and the Palatine Germans up the Shenandoah Valley into the western part of Virginia, and along the Piedmont region of the Carolinas.[4] The Germans in New York pushed the frontier of settlement up the Mohawk to German Flats.[5] In Pennsylvania the town of Bedford indicates the line of settlement. Settlements had begun on New River, a branch of the Kanawha, and on the sources of the Yadkin and French Broad.[6] The King attempted to arrest the advance by his proclamation of 1763,[7] forbidding settlements beyond the sources of the rivers flowing into the Atlantic; but in vain. In the period of the Revolution the frontier crossed the Alleghanies into Kentucky and Tennessee, and the upper waters of the Ohio were settled.[8] When the first census was taken in 1790, the continuous settled area was bounded by a line which ran near the coast of Maine, and included New England except a portion of Vermont and New Hampshire, New York along the Hudson and up the Mohawk about Schenectady, eastern and southern Pennsylvania, Virginia well across the Shenandoah Valley, and the Carolinas and eastern Georgia.[9] Beyond this region of continuous settlement were the small settled areas of Kentucky and Tennessee, and the Ohio, with the mountains intervening between them and the Atlantic area, thus giving a new and important character to the frontier. The isolation of the region increased its peculiarly American tendencies, and the need of transportation facilities to connect it with the East called out important schemes of internal improvement, which will be noted farther on. The "West," as a self-conscious section, began to evolve.

From decade to decade distinct advances of the frontier occurred. By the census of 1820[10] the settled area included Ohio, southern Indiana and Illinois, southeastern Missouri, and about one-half of Louisiana. This settled area had surrounded Indian areas, and the management of these tribes became an object of political concern. The frontier region of the time lay along the Great Lakes, where Astor's American Fur Company operated in the Indian trade,[11] and beyond the Mississippi, where Indian traders extended their activity even to the Rocky Mountains; Florida also furnished frontier conditions. The Mississippi River region was the scene of typical frontier settlements.[12]

The rising steam navigation[13] on western waters, the opening of the Erie Canal, and the westward extension of cotton[14] culture added five frontier states to the Union in this period. Grund, writing in 1836, declares: "It appears then that the universal disposition of Americans to emigrate to the western wilderness, in order to enlarge their dominion over inanimate nature, is the actual result of an expansive power which is inherent in them, and which by continually agitating all classes of society is constantly throwing a large portion of the whole population on the extreme confines of the State, in order to gain space for its development. Hardly is a new State or Territory formed before the same principle manifests itself again and gives rise to a further emigration; and so is it destined to go on until a physical barrier must finally obstruct its progress."[15]

In the middle of this century the line indicated by the present eastern boundary of Indian Territory, Nebraska, and Kansas marked the frontier of the Indian country.[16] Minnesota and Wisconsin still exhibited frontier conditions,[17] but the distinctive frontier of the period is found in California, where the gold discoveries had sent a sudden tide of adventurous miners, and in Oregon, and the settlements in Utah.[18] As the frontier has leaped over the Alleghanies, so now it skipped the Great Plains and the Rocky Mountains; and in the same way that the advance of the frontiersmen beyond the Alleghanies had caused the rise of important questions of transportation and internal improvement, so now the settlers beyond the Rocky Mountains needed means of communication with the East, and in the furnishing of these arose the settlement of the Great Plains and the development of still another kind of frontier life. Railroads, fostered by land grants, sent an increasing tide of immigrants into the far West. The United States Army fought a series of Indian wars in Minnesota, Dakota, and the Indian Territory.

By 1880 the settled area had been pushed into northern Michigan, Wisconsin, and Minnesota, along Dakota rivers, and in the Black Hills region, and was ascending the rivers of Kansas and Nebraska. The development of mines in Colorado had drawn isolated frontier settlements into that region, and Montana and Idaho were receiving settlers. The frontier was found in these mining camps and the ranches of the Great Plains. The superintendent of the census for 1890 reports, as previously stated, that the settlements of the West lie so scattered over the region that there can no longer be said to be a frontier line.

In these successive frontiers we find natural boundary lines which have served to mark and to affect the characteristics of the frontiers, namely: The "fall line;" the Alleghany Mountains; the Mississippi; the Missouri, where its direction approximates north and south; the line of the arid lands, approximately the ninety-ninth meridian; and the Rocky Mountains. The fall line marked the frontier of the seventeenth century; the Alleghanies that of the eighteenth; the Mississippi that of the first quarter of the nineteenth; the Missouri that of the middle of this century (omitting the California movement); and the belt of the Rocky Mountains and the arid tract, the present frontier. Each was won by a series of Indian wars.

The Frontier Furnishes a Field for
Comparative Study of Social Development

At the Atlantic frontier one can study the germs of processes repeated at each successive frontier. We have the complex European life sharply precipitated by the wilderness into the simplicity of primitive conditions. The first frontier had to meet its Indian question, its question of the disposition of the public domain, of the means of intercourse with older settlements, of the extension of political organization, of religious and educational activity. And the settlement of these and similar questions for one frontier served as a guide for the next. The American student needs not to go to the "prim little townships of Sleswick" for illustrations of the law of continuity and development. For example, he may study the origin of our land policies in the colonial land policy; he may see how the system grew by adapting the statutes to the customs of the successive frontiers.[19] He may see how the mining experience in the lead regions of Wisconsin, Illinois, and Iowa was applied to the mining laws of the Rockies,[20] and how our Indian policy has been a series of experimentations on successive frontiers. Each tier of new States has found in the older ones material for its constitutions.[21] Each frontier has made similar contributions to American character, as will be discussed farther on.

But with all these similarities there are essential differences, due to the place element and the time element. It is evident that the farming frontier of the Mississippi Valley presents different conditions from the mining frontier of the Rocky Mountains. The frontier reached by the Pacific Railroad, surveyed into rectangles, guarded by the United States Army, and recruited by the daily immigrant ship, moves forward at a swifter pace and in a different way than the frontier reached by the birch canoe or the pack horse. The geologist traces patiently the shores of ancient seas, maps their areas, and compares the older and the newer. It would be a work worth the historian's labors to mark these various frontiers and in detail compare one with another. Not only would there result a more adequate conception of American development and characteristics, but invaluable additions would be made to the history of society.

Loria,[22] the Italian economist, has urged the study of colonial life as an aid in understanding the stages of European development, affirming that colonial settlement is for economic science what the mountain is for geology, bringing to light primitive stratifications. "America," he says, "has the key to the historical enigma which Europe has sought for centuries in vain, and the land which has no history reveals luminously the course of universal history." There is much truth in this. The United States lies like a huge page in the history of society. Line by line as we read this continental page from west to east we find the record of social evolution. It begins with the

Indian and the hunter; it goes on to tell of the disintegration of savagery by the entrance of the trader, the pathfinder of civilization; we read the annals of the pastoral stage in ranch life; the exploitation of the soil by the raising of unrotated crops of corn and wheat in sparsely settled farming communities; the intensive culture of the denser farm settlement; and finally the manufacturing organization with city and factory system.[23] This page is familiar to the student of census statistics, but how little of it has been used by our historians. Particularly in eastern States this page is a palimpsest. What is now a manufacturing State was in an earlier decade an area of intensive farming. Earlier yet it had been a wheat area, and still earlier the "range" had attracted the cattle-herder. Thus Wisconsin, now developing manufacture, is a State with varied agricultural interests. But earlier it was given over to almost exclusive grain-raising, like North Dakota at the present time.

Each of these areas has had an influence in our economic and political history; the evolution of each into a higher stage has worked political transformations. But what constitutional historian has made any adequate attempt to interpret political facts by the light of these social areas and changes?[24]

The Atlantic frontier was compounded of fisherman, fur-trader, miner, cattle-raiser, and farmer. Excepting the fisherman, each type of industry was on the march toward the West, impelled by an irresistible attraction. Each passed in successive waves across the continent. Stand at Cumberland Gap and watch the procession of civilization, marching single file — the buffalo following the trail to the salt springs, the Indian, the fur-trader and hunter, the cattle-raiser, the pioneer farmer — and the frontier has passed by. Stand at South Pass in the Rockies a century later and see the same procession with wider intervals between. The unequal rate of advance compels us to distinguish the frontier into the trader's frontier, the rancher's frontier, or the miner's frontier, and the farmer's frontier. When the mines and the cow pens were still near the fall line the traders' pack trains were tinkling across the Alleghanies, and the French on the Great Lakes were fortifying their posts, alarmed by the British trader's birch canoe. When the trappers scaled the Rockies, the farmer was still near the mouth of the Missouri.

The Indian Trader's Frontier

Why was it that the Indian trader passed so rapidly across the continent? What effects followed from the trader's frontier? The trade was coeval with American discovery. The Norsemen, Vespuccius, Verrazani, Hudson, John Smith, all trafficked for furs. The Plymouth pilgrims settled in Indian corn-fields, and their first return cargo was of beaver and lumber. The records of the various New England colonies show how steadily exploration was carried into the wilderness by this trade. What is true for New England is, as would be expected, even plainer for the rest of the colonies. All along the coast from Maine to Georgia the Indian trade opened up the river courses. Steadily the trader passed westward, utilizing the older lines of French trade. The Ohio, the Great Lakes, the Mississippi, the Missouri, and the Platte, the lines of western advance, were ascended by traders. They found the passes in the Rocky Mountains and guided Lewis and Clark,[25] Fremont, and Bidwell. The explanation of the rapidity of this advance is connected with the effects of the trader on the Indian. The trading post left the unarmed tribes at the mercy of those that had purchased fire-arms — a truth which the Iroquois Indians wrote in blood, and so the remote and unvisited tribes gave eager welcome to the trader. "The savages," wrote La Salle, "take better care of us French than of their own children; from us only can they get guns and goods." This accounts for the trader's power and the rapidity of his advance. Thus the disintegrating forces of civilization entered the wilderness. Every river valley and Indian trail became a fissure in Indian society, and so that society became honeycombed. Long before the pioneer farmer appeared on the scene, primitive Indian life had passed away. The farmers met Indians armed with guns. The trading frontier, while steadily undermining Indian power by making the tribes ultimately dependent on the whites, yet, through its sale of guns, gave to the Indians increased power of resistance to the farming frontier. French colonization was dominated by its trading frontier; English colonization by its farming frontier. There was an antagonism between the two frontiers as between the two nations. Said Duquesne to the Iroquois, "Are you ignorant of the difference between the king of England and the king of France? Go see the forts that our king has established and you will see that you can still hunt under their very walls. They have been placed for your advantage in places which you frequent. The English, on the contrary, are no sooner in possession of a place than the game is driven away. The forest falls before them as they advance, and the soil is laid bare so that you can scarce find the wherewithal to erect a shelter for the night."

And yet, in spite of this opposition of the interests of the trader and the farmer, the Indian trade pioneered the way for civilization. The buffalo trail became the Indian trail, and this because the trader's "trace;" the trails widened into roads, and the roads into turnpikes, and these in turn were transformed into railroads. The same origin can be shown for the railroads of the South, the far West, and the Dominion of Canada.[26] The trading posts reached by these trails were on the sites of Indian villages which had been placed in positions suggested by nature; and these trading posts, situated so as to command the water systems of the country, have grown into such cities as Albany, Pittsburg, Detroit, Chicago, St. Louis, Council Bluffs, and Kansas

City. Thus civilization in America has followed the arteries made by geology, pouring an ever richer tide through them, until at last the slender paths of aboriginal intercourse have been broadened and interwoven into the complex mazes of modern commercial lines; the wilderness has been interpenetrated by lines of civilization growing ever more numerous. It is like the steady growth of a complex nervous system for the originally simple, inert continent. If one would understand why we are to-day one nation, rather than a collection of isolated states, he must study this economic and social consolidation of the country. In this progress from savage conditions lie topics for the evolutionist.[27]

The effect of the Indian frontier as a consolidating agent in our history is important. From the close of the seventeenth century various intercolonial congresses have been called to treat with Indians and establish common measures of defense. Particularism was strongest in colonies with no Indian frontier. This frontier stretched along the western border like a cord of union. The Indian was a common danger, demanding united action. Most celebrated of these conferences was the Albany congress of 1754, called to treat with the Six Nations, and to consider plans of union. Even a cursory reading of the plan proposed by the congress reveals the importance of the frontier. The powers of the general council and the officers were, chiefly, the determination of peace and war with the Indians, the regulation of Indian trade, the purchase of Indian lands, and the creation and government of new settlements as a security against the Indians. It is evident that the unifying tendencies of the Revolutionary period were facilitated by the previous cooperation in the regulation of the frontier. In this connection may be mentioned the importance of the frontier, from that day to this, as a military training school, keeping alive the power of resistance to aggression, and developing the stalwart and rugged qualities of the frontiersman.

The Rancher's Frontier

It would not be possible in the limits of this paper to trace the other frontiers across the continent. Travelers of the eighteenth century found the "cowpens" among the canebrakes and peavine pastures of the South, and the "cow drivers" took their droves to Charleston, Philadelphia, and New York.[28] Travelers at the close of the War of 1812 met droves of more than a thousand cattle and swine from the interior of Ohio going to Pennsylvania to fatten for the Philadelphia market.[29] The ranges of the Great Plains, with ranch and cowboy and nomadic life, are things of yesterday and of to-day. The experience of the Carolina cowpens guided the ranchers of Texas. One element favoring the rapid extension of the rancher's frontier is the fact that in a remote country lacking transportation facilities the product must be in small bulk, or must be able to transport itself, and the cattle raiser could easily drive this product to market. The effect of these great ranches on the subsequent agrarian history of the localities in which they existed should be studied.

The Farmer's Frontier

The maps of the census reports show an uneven advance of the farmer's frontier, with tongues of settlement pushed forward and with indentations of wilderness. In part this is due to Indian resistance, in part to the location of river valleys and passes, in part to the unequal force of the centers of frontier attraction. Among the important centers of attraction may be mentioned the following: fertile and favorably situated soils, salt springs, mines, and army posts.

ARMY POSTS

The frontier army post, serving to protect the settlers from the Indians, has also acted as a wedge to open the Indian country, and has been a nucleus for settlement.[30] In this connection mention should also be made of the Government military and exploring expeditions in determining the lines of settlement. But all the more important expeditions were greatly indebted to the earliest pathmakers, the Indian guides, the traders and trappers, and the French voyageurs, who were inevitable parts of governmental expeditions from the days of Lewis and Clark.[31] Each expedition was an epitome of the previous factors in western advance.

SALT SPRINGS

In an interesting monograph, Victor Hehn[32] has traced the effect of salt upon early European development, and has pointed out how it affected the lines of settlement and the form of administration. A similar study might be made for the salt springs of the United States. The early settlers were tied to the coast by the need of salt, without which they could not preserve their meats or live in comfort. Writing in 1752, Bishop Spangenburg says of a colony for which he was seeking lands in North Carolina, "They will require salt & other necessaries which they can neither manufacture nor raise. Either they must go to Charleston, which is 300 miles distant . . . Or else they must go to Boling's Point in V^a on a branch of the James & is also 300 miles from here . . . Or else they must go down the Roanoke —I know not how many miles—where salt is brought up from the Cape Fear."[33] This may serve as a typical illustration. An annual pilgrimage to the coast for salt thus became essential. Taking flocks or furs and ginseng root, the early settlers sent their pack trains after seeding time each year to the coast.[34] This proved to be an important educational influence, since it was almost the only way in which the pioneer learned what was going on in the East. But when discovery was made of the salt springs of the Kanawha, and the Holston, and Kentucky, and central New York, the West began to be freed from dependence on the coast. It was in part the effect of finding these salt springs that enabled settlement to cross the mountains.

From the time the mountains rose between the pioneer and the seaboard, a new order of Americanism arose. The West and the East began to get out of touch of each other. The settlements from the sea to the mountains kept connection with the rear and had a certain solidarity. But the over-mountain men grew more and more independent. The East took a narrow view of American advance, and nearly lost these men. Kentucky and Tennessee history bears abundant witness to the truth of this statement. The East began to try to hedge and limit westward expansion. Though Webster could declare that there were no Alleghanies in his politics, yet in politics in general they were a very solid factor.

LAND

The exploitation of the beasts took hunter and trader to the west, the exploitation of the grasses took the rancher west, and the exploitation of the virgin soil of the river valleys and prairies attracted the farmer. Good soils have been the most continuous attraction to the farmer's frontier. The land hunger of the Virginians drew them down the rivers into Carolina, in early colonial days; the search for soils took the Massachusetts men to Pennsylvania and to New York. As the eastern lands were taken up migration flowed across them to the west. Daniel Boone, the great backwoodsman, who combined the occupations of hunter, trader, cattle-raiser, farmer, and surveyor — learning, probably from the traders, of the fertility of the lands on the upper Yadkin, where the traders were wont to rest as they took their way to the Indians, left his Pennsylvania home with his father, and passed down the Great Valley road to that stream. Learning from a trader whose posts were on the Red River in Kentucky of its game and rich pastures, he pioneered the way for the farmers to that region. Thence he passed to the frontier of Missouri, where his settlement was long a landmark on the frontier. Here again he helped to open the way for civilization, finding salt licks, and trails, and land. His son was among the earliest trappers in the passes of the Rocky Mountains, and his party are said to have been the first to camp on the present site of Denver. His grandson, Col. A. J. Boone, of Colorado, was a power among the Indians of the Rocky Mountains, and was appointed an agent by the Government. Kit Carson's mother was a Boone.[35] Thus this family epitomizes the backwoodsman's advance across the continent.

The farmer's advance came in a distinct series of waves. In Peck's New Guide to the West, published in Boston in 1837, occurs this suggestive passage:

Generally, in all the western settlements, three classes, like the waves of the ocean, have rolled one after the other. First comes the pioneer, who depends for the subsistence of his family chiefly upon the natural growth of vegetation, called the "range," and the proceeds of hunting. His implements of agriculture are rude, chiefly of his own make, and his efforts directed mainly to a crop of corn and a "truck patch." The last is a rude garden for growing cabbage, beans, corn for roasting ears, cucumbers, and potatoes. A log cabin, and, occasionally, a stable and corn-crib, and a field of a dozen acres, the timber girdled or "deadened," and fenced, are enough for his occupancy. It is quite immaterial whether he ever becomes the owner of the soil. He is the occupant for the time being, pays no rent, and feels as independent as the "lord of the manor." With a horse, cow, and one or two breeders of swine, he strikes into the woods with his family, and becomes the founder of a new county, or perhaps state. He builds his cabin, gathers around him a few other families of similar tastes and habits, and occupies till the range is somewhat subdued, and hunting a little precarious, or, which is more frequently the case, till the neighbors crowd around, roads, bridges, and fields annoy him, and he lacks elbow room. The preemption law enables him to dispose of his cabin and cornfield to the next class of emigrants; and, to employ his own figures, he "breaks for the high timber," "clears out for the New Purchase," or migrates to Arkansas or Texas, to work the same process over.

The next class of emigrants purchase the lands, add field to field, clear out the roads, throw rough bridges over the streams, put up hewn log houses with glass windows and brick or stone chimneys, occasionally plant orchards, build mills, schoolhouses, court-houses, etc., and exhibit the picture and forms of plain, frugal, civilized life.

Another wave rolls on. The men of capital and enterprise come. The settler is ready to sell out and take the advantage of the rise in property, push farther into the interior and become, himself, a man of capital and enterprise in turn. The small village rises to a spacious town or city; substantial edifices of brick, extensive fields, orchards, gardens, colleges, and churches are seen. Broadcloths, silks, leghorns, crapes, and all the refinements, luxuries, elegancies, frivolities, and fashions are in vogue. Thus wave after wave is rolling westward; the real Eldorado is still farther on.

A portion of the two first classes remain stationary amidst the general movement, improve their habits and condition, and rise in the scale of society.

The writer has traveled much amongst the first class, the real pioneers. He has lived many years in connection with the second grade; and now the third wave is sweeping over large districts of Indiana, Illinois, and Missouri. Migration has become almost a habit in the West. Hundreds of men can be found, not over 50 years of age, who have settled for the fourth, fifth, or sixth time on a new spot. To sell out and remove only a few hundred miles makes up a portion of the variety of backwoods life and manners.[36]

Omitting those of the pioneer farmers who move from the love of adventure, the advance of the more steady farmer is easy to understand. Obviously the immigrant was attracted by the cheap lands of the frontier, and even the native farmer felt their influence strongly. Year by year the farmers who lived on soil whose returns were diminished by unrotated crops were offered the virgin soil of the frontier at nominal prices. Their growing families demanded more lands, and these were dear. The competition of the unexhausted, cheap, and easily tilled prairie lands compelled the farmer either to go west and continue the exhaustion of the soil on a new frontier, or to adopt intensive culture. Thus the census of 1890 shows, in the Northwest, many counties in which there is an absolute or a relative decrease of population. These States have been sending farmers to advance the frontier on the plains, and have themselves begun to turn to intensive farming and to manufacture. A decade before this, Ohio had shown the same transition stage. Thus the demand for land and the love of wilderness freedom drew the frontier ever onward.

Having now roughly outlined the various kinds of frontiers, and their modes of advance, chiefly from the point of view of the frontier itself, we may next inquire what were the influences on the East and on the Old World. A rapid enumeration of some of the more noteworthy effects is all that I have time for.

Composite Nationality

First, we note that the frontier promoted the formation of a composite nationality for the American people. The coast was preponderantly English, but the later tides of continental immigration flowed across to the free lands. This was the case from the early colonial days. The Scotch Irish and the Palatine Germans, or "Pennsylvania Dutch," furnished the dominant element in the stock of the colonial frontier. With these peoples were also the freed indented servants, or redemptioners, who at the expiration of their time of service passed to the frontier. Governor Spotswood of Virginia writes in 1717, "The inhabitants of our frontiers are composed generally of such as have been transported hither as servants, and, being out of their time, settle themselves where land is to be taken up and that will produce the necessarys of life with little labour."[37] Very generally these redemptioners were of non-English stock. In the crucible of the frontier the immigrants were Americanized, liberated, and fused into a mixed race, English in neither nationality or characteristics. The process has gone on from the early days to our own. Burke and other writers in the middle of the eighteenth century believed that Pennsylvania[38] was "threatened with the danger of being wholly foreign in language, manner, and perhaps even inclinations." The German and Scotch-Irish elements in the frontier of the South were only less great. In the middle of the present century the German element in Wisconsin was already so considerable that leading publicists looked to the creation of a German state out of the commonwealth by concentrating their colonization.[39] Such examples teach us to beware of misinterpreting the fact that there is a common English speech in America into a belief that the stock is also English.

Industrial Independence

In another way the advance of the frontier decreased our dependence on England. The coast, particularly of the South, lacked diversified industries, and was dependent on England for the bulk of its supplies. In the South there was even a dependence on the Northern colonies for articles of food. Governor Glenn, of South Carolina, writes in the middle of the eighteenth century: "Our trade with New York and Philadelphia was of this sort, draining us of all the little money and bills we could gather from other places for their bread, flour, beer, hams, bacon, and other things of their produce, all which, except beer, our new townships begin to supply us with, which are settled with very industrious and thriving Germans. This no doubt diminishes the number of shipping and the appearance of our trade, but it is far from being a detriment to us."[40] Before long the frontier created a demand for merchants. As it retreated from the coast it became less and less possible for England to bring her supplies directly to the consumer's wharf, and carry away staple crops, and staple crops began to give way to diversified agriculture for a time. The effect of this phase of the frontier action upon the northern section is perceived when we realize how the advance of the frontier aroused seaboard cities like Boston, New York, and Baltimore, to engage in rivalry for what Washington called "the extensive and valuable trade of a rising empire."

Effects on National Legislation

The legislation which most developed the powers of the National Government, and played the largest part in its activity, was conditioned on the frontier. Writers have discussed the subjects of tariff, land, and internal improvement, as subsidiary to the slavery question. But when American history comes to be rightly viewed it will be seen that the slavery question is an incident. In the period from the end of the first half of the present century to the close of the civil war slavery rose to primary, but far from exclusive, importance. But this does not justify Dr. von Holst (to take an example) in treating our constitutional history in its formative period down to 1828 in a single volume, giving six volumes chiefly to the history of slavery from 1828 to 1861, under the title "Constitutional History of the United States." The growth of nationalism and the evolution of American political institutions were dependent on the advance of the frontier. Even so recent a writer as Rhodes, in his History of the United States since the compromise of 1850, has treated the legislation called out by the western advance as incidental to the slavery struggle.

This is a wrong perspective. The pioneer needed the goods of the coast, and so the grand series of internal improvement and railroad legislation began, with potent nationalizing effects. Over internal improvements occurred great debates, in which grave constitutional questions were discussed. Sectional groupings appear in the votes, profoundly significant for the historian. Loose construction increased as the nation marched westward.[41] But the West was not content with bringing the farm to the factory. Under the lead of Clay — "Harry of the West" — protective tariffs were passed, with the cry of bringing the factory to the farm. The disposition of the public lands was a third important subject of national legislation influenced by the frontier.

The Public Domain

The public domain has been a force of profound importance in the nationalization and development of the Government. The effects of the struggle of the landed and the landless States, and of the ordinance of 1787,* need no discussion.[42] Administratively the frontier called out some of the highest and most vitalizing activities of the General Government. The purchase of Louisiana was perhaps the constitutional turning point in the history of the Republic, inasmuch as it afforded both a new area for national legislation and the occasion of the downfall of the policy of strict construction. But the purchase of Louisiana was called out by frontier needs and demands. As frontier States accrued to the Union the national power grew. In a speech on the dedication of the Calhoun monument Mr. Lamar explained: "In

---

Land Ordinance of 1787. This landmark legislation organized open territory north of present-day Ohio, stipulating the steps by which frontier areas moved through territorial stages to statehood.

1789 the States were the creators of the Federal Government; in 1861 the Federal Government was the creator of a large majority of the States."

When we consider the public domain from the point of view of the sale and disposal of the public lands we are again brought face to face with the frontier. The policy of the United States in dealing with its lands is in sharp contrast with the European system of scientific administration. Efforts to make this domain a source of revenue, and to withhold it from emigrants in order that settlement might be compact, were in vain. The jealousy and the fears of the East were powerless in the face of the demands of the frontiersmen. John Quincy Adams was obliged to confess: "My own system of administration, which was to make the national domain the inexhaustible fund for progressive and unceasing internal improvement, has failed." The reason is obvious; a system of administration was not what the West demanded; it wanted land. Adams states the situation as follows: "The slaveholders of the South have bought the cooperation of the western country by the bribe of the western lands, abandoning to the new Western States their own proportion of the public property and aiding them in the design of grasping all the lands into their own hands. Thomas H. Benton was the author of this system, which he brought forward as a substitute for the American system of Mr. Clay, and to supplant him as the leading statesman of the West. Mr. Clay, by his tariff compromise with Mr. Calhoun, abandoned his own American system. At the same time he brought forward a plan for distributing among all the States of the Union the proceeds of the sales of the public lands. His bill for that purpose passed both Houses of Congress, but was vetoed by President Jackson, who, in his annual message of December, 1832, formally recommended that all public lands should be gratuitously given away to individual adventurers and to the States in which the lands are situated."[43]

"No subject," said Henry Clay, "which has presented itself to the present, or perhaps any preceding, Congress, is of greater magnitude than that of the public lands." When we consider the far-reaching effects of the Government's land policy upon political, economic, and social aspects of American life, we are disposed to agree with him. But this legislation was framed under frontier influences, and under the lead of Western statesmen like Benton and Jackson. Said Senator Scott of Indiana in 1841: "I consider the preemption law merely declaratory of the custom or common law of the settlers."

National Tendencies of the Frontier

It is safe to say that the legislation with regard to land, tariff, and internal improvements — the American system of the nationalizing Whig party — was conditioned on frontier ideas and needs. But it was not merely in legislative action that the frontier worked against the sectionalism of the coast. The economic and social characteristics of the frontier worked against sectionalism. The men of the frontier had closer resemblances to the Middle region than to either of the other sections. Pennsylvania had been the seed-plot of frontier emigration, and, although she passed on her settlers along the Great Valley into the west of Virginia and the Carolinas, yet the industrial society of these Southern frontiersmen was always more like that of the Middle region than like that of the tide-water portion of the South, which later came to spread its industrial type throughout the South.

The Middle region, entered by New York harbor, was an open door to all Europe. The tide-water part of the South represented typical Englishmen, modified by a warm climate and servile labor, and living in baronial fashion on great plantations; New England stood for a special English movement — Puritanism. The Middle region was less English than the other sections. It had a wide mixture of nationalities, a varied society, the mixed town and county system of local government, a varied economic life, many religious sects. In short, it was a region mediating between New England and the South, and the East and the West. It represented that composite nationality which the contemporary United States exhibits, that juxtaposition of non-English groups, occupying a valley or a little settlement, and presenting reflections of the map of Europe in their variety. It was democratic and non-sectional, if not national; "easy, tolerant, and contented;" rooted strongly in material prosperity. It was typical of the modern United States. It was least sectional, not only because it lay between North and South, but also because with no barriers to shut out its frontiers from its settled region, and with a system of connecting waterways, the Middle region mediated between East and West as well as between North and South. Thus it became the typically American region. Even the New Englander, who was shut out from the frontier by the Middle region, tarrying in New York or Pennsylvania on his westward march, lost the acuteness of his sectionalism on the way.[44]

The spread of cotton culture into the interior of the South finally broke down the contrast between the "tide-water" region and the rest of the State, and based Southern interests on slavery. Before this process revealed its results the western portion of the South, which was akin to Pennsylvania in stock, society, and industry, showed tendencies to fall away from the faith of the fathers into internal improvement legislation and nationalism. In the Virginia convention of 1829–'30, called to revise the constitution, Mr. Leigh, of Chesterfield, one of the tide-water counties, declared:

> One of the main causes of discontent which led to this convention, that which had the strongest influence in overcoming our veneration for the work of

our fathers, which taught us to contemn the sentiments of Henry and Mason and Pendleton, which weaned us from our reverence for the constituted authorities of the State, was an overweening passion for internal improvement. I say this with perfect knowledge, for it has been avowed to me by gentlemen from the West over and over again. And let me tell the gentleman from Albemarle (Mr. Gordon) that it has been another principal object of those who set this ball of revolution in motion, to overturn the doctrine of State rights, of which Virginia has been the very pillar, and to remove the barrier she has interposed to the interference of the Federal Government in that same work of internal improvement, by so reorganizing the legislature that Virginia, too, may be hitched to the Federal car.

It was this nationalizing tendency of the West that transformed the democracy of Jefferson into the national republicanism of Monroe and the democracy of Andrew Jackson. The West of the war of 1812, the West of Clay, and Benton, and Harrison, and Andrew Jackson, shut off by the Middle States and the mountains from the coast sections, had a solidarity of its own with national tendencies.[45] On the tide of the Father of Waters, North and South met and mingled into a nation. Interstate migration went steadily on — a process of cross-fertilization of ideas and institutions. The fierce struggle of the sections over slavery on the western frontier does not diminish the truth of this statement; it proves the truth of it. Slavery was a sectional trait that would not down, but in the West it could not remain sectional. It was the greatest of frontiersmen who declared: "I believe this Government can not endure permanently half slave and half free. It will become all of one thing or all of the other." Nothing works for nationalism like intercourse within the nation. Mobility of population is death to localism, and the western frontier worked irresistibly in unsettling population. The effects reached back from the frontier and affected profoundly the Atlantic coast and even the Old World.

Growth of Democracy

But the most important effect of the frontier has been in the promotion of democracy here and in Europe. As has been indicated, the frontier is productive of individualism. Complex society is precipitated by the wilderness into a kind of primitive organization based on the family. The tendency is anti-social. It produces antipathy to control, and particularly to any direct control. The tax-gatherer is viewed as a representative of oppression. Prof. Osgood, in an able article,[46] has pointed out that the frontier conditions prevalent in the colonies are important factors in the explanation of the American Revolution, where individual liberty was sometimes confused with absence of all effective government. The same conditions aid in explaining the difficulty of instituting a strong government in the period of the confederacy. The frontier individualism has from the beginning promoted democracy.

The frontier States that came into the Union in the first quarter of a century of its existence came in with democratic suffrage provisions, and had reactive effects of the highest importance upon the older States whose peoples were being attracted there. An extension of the franchise became essential. It was *western* New York that forced an extension of suffrage in the constitutional convention of that State in 1821; and it was *western* Virginia that compelled the tide-water region to put a more liberal suffrage provision in the constitution framed in 1830, and to give to the frontier region a more nearly proportionate representation with the tide-water aristocracy. The rise of democracy as an effective force in the nation came in with western preponderance under Jackson and William Henry Harrison, and it meant the triumph of the frontier — with all of its good and with all of its evil elements.[47] An interesting illustration of the tone of frontier democracy in 1830 comes from the same debates in the Virginia convention already referred to. A representative from western Virginia declared:

> But, sir, it is not the increase of population in the West which this gentleman ought to fear. It is the energy which the mountain breeze and western habits impart to those emigrants. They are regenerated, politically I mean, sir. They soon become *working politicians;* and the difference, sir, between a *talking* and a *working* politican is immense. The Old Dominion has long been celebrated for producing great orators; the ablest metaphysicians in policy; men that can split hairs in all abstruse questions of political economy. But at home, or when they return from Congress, they have negroes to fan them asleep. But a Pennsylvania, a New York, an Ohio, or a western Virginia statesman, though far inferior in logic, metaphysics, and rhetoric to an old Virginia statesman, has this advantage, that when he returns home he takes off his coat and takes hold of the plow. This gives him bone and muscle, sir, and preserves his republican principles pure and uncontaminated.

So long as free land exists, the opportunity for a competency exists, and economic power secures political power. But the democracy born of free land, strong in selfishness and individualism, intolerant of administrative experience and education, and pressing individual liberty beyond its proper bounds, has its dangers as well as its benefits. Individualism in America has allowed a laxity in regard to governmental affairs which has rendered possible the spoils system and all the manifest evils that follow from the lack of a highly developed civic spirit. In this connection may be noted also the influence of frontier conditions in permitting lax business honor, inflated paper currency and wild-cat banking. The colonial and revolutionary frontier was the region whence emanated many of the worst forms of an evil currency.[48] The West in the war of 1812 repeated the phenomenon on the frontier of that day, while the speculation and wild-cat banking of the period of the crisis of 1837 occurred on the new frontier belt of the next tier of States. Thus each one of the periods of lax financial integrity coincides with periods when a new set of frontier communities had arisen, and coincides in area with these successive frontiers, for the most part. The recent Populist agitation is a case in point. Many a State that now declines any connection with the tenets of the Populists, itself adhered to such ideas in an earlier stage of the development of the State. A primitive society can hardly be expected to show the intelligent appreciation of the complexity of business interests in a developed society. The continual recurrence of these areas of paper-money agitation is another evidence that the frontier can be isolated and studied as a factor in American history of the highest importance.[49]

Attempts to Check and Regulate the Frontier

The East has always feared the result of an unregulated advance of the frontier, and has tried to check and guide it. The English authorities would have checked settlement at the headwaters of the Atlantic tributaries and allowed the "savages to enjoy their deserts in quiet lest the peltry trade should decrease." This called out Burke's splendid protest:

> If you stopped your grants, what would be the consequence? The people would occupy without grants. They have already so occupied in many places. You can not station garrisons in every part of these deserts. If you drive the people from one place, they will carry on their annual tillage and remove with their flocks and herds to another. Many of the people in the back settlements are already little attached to particular situations. Already they have topped the Appalachian mountains. From thence they behold before them an immense plain, one vast, rich, level meadow; a square of five hundred miles. Over this they would wander without a possibility of restraint; they would change their manners with their habits of life; would soon forget a government by which they were disowned; would become hordes of English Tartars; and, pouring down upon your unfortified frontiers a fierce and irresistible cavalry, become masters of your governors and your counselors, your collectors and comptrollers, and of all the slaves that adhered to them. Such would, and in no long time must, be the effect of attempting to forbid as a crime and to suppress as an evil the command and blessing of Providence, "Increase and multiply." Such would be the happy result of an endeavor to

keep as a lair of wild beasts that earth which God, by an express charter, has given to the children of men.

But the English Government was not alone in its desire to limit the advance of the frontier and guide its destinies. Tide-water Virginia[50] and South Carolina[51] gerrymandered those colonies to insure the dominance of the coast in their legislatures. Washington desired to settle a State at a time in the Northwest; Jefferson would reserve from settlement the territory of his Louisiana purchase north of the thirty-second parallel, in order to offer it to the Indians in exchange for their settlements east of the Mississippi. "When we shall be full on this side," he writes, "we may lay off a range of States on the Western bank from the head to the mouth, and so range after range, advancing compactly as we multiply." Madison went so far as to argue to the French minister that the United States had no interest in seeing population extend itself on the right bank of the Mississippi, but should rather fear it. When the Oregon question was under debate, in 1824, Smyth, of Virginia, would draw an unchangeable line for the limits of the United States at the outer limit of two tiers of States beyond the Mississippi, complaining that the seaboard States were being drained of the flower of their population by the bringing of too much land into market. Even Thomas Benton, the man of widest views of the destiny of the West, at this stage of his career declared that along the ridge of the Rocky mountains "the western limits of the Republic should be drawn, and the statue of the fabled god Terminus should be raised upon its highest peak, never to be thrown down."[52] But the attempts to limit the boundaries, to restrict land sales and settlement, and to deprive the West of its share of political power were all in vain. Steadily the frontier of settlement advanced and carried with it individualism, democracy, and nationalism, and powerfully affected the East and the Old World.

Missionary Activity

The most effective efforts of the East to regulate the frontier came through its educational and religious activity, exerted by interstate migration and by organized societies. Speaking in 1835, Dr. Lyman Beecher declared: "It is equally plain that the religious and political destiny of our nation is to be decided in the West," and he pointed out that the population of the West "is assembled from all the States of the Union and from all the nations of Europe, and is rushing in like the waters of the flood, demanding for its moral preservation the immediate and universal action of those institutions which discipline the mind and arm the conscience and the heart. And so various are the opinions and habits, and so recent and imperfect is the acquaintance, and so sparse are the settlements of the West, that no homogeneous public sentiment can be formed to legislate immediately into being the requisite institutions. And yet they are all needed immediately in their utmost perfection and power. A nation is being 'born in a day.' . . . But what will become of the West if her prosperity rushes up to such a majesty of power, while those great institutions linger which are necessary to form the mind and the conscience and the heart of that vast world. It must not be permitted. . . . Let no man at the East quiet himself and dream of liberty, whatever may become of the West. . . . Her destiny is our destiny."[53]

With the appeal to the conscience of New England, he adds appeals to her fears lest other religious sects anticipate her own. The New England preacher and school-teacher left their mark on the West. The dread of Western emancipation from New England's political and economic control was parralled by her fears lest the West cut loose from her religion. Commenting in 1850 on reports that settlement was rapidly extending northward in Wisconsin, the editor of the Home Missionary writes: "We scarcely know whether to rejoice or mourn over this extension of our settlements. While we sympathize in whatever tends to increase the physical resources and prosperity of our country, we can not forget that with all these dispersions into remote and still remoter corners of the land the supply of the means of grace is becoming relatively less and less." Acting in accordance with such ideas, home missions were established and Western colleges were erected. As seaboard cities like Philadelphia, New York, and Baltimore strove for the mastery of Western trade, so the various denominations strove for the possession of the West. Thus an intellectual stream from New England sources fertilized the West. Other sections sent their missionaries; but the real struggle was between sects. The contest for power and the expansive tendency furnished to the various sects by the existence of a moving frontier must have had important results on the character of religious organization in the United States. The multiplication of rival churches in the little frontier towns had deep and lasting social effects. The religious aspects of the frontier make a chapter in our history which needs study.

Intellectual Traits

From the conditions of frontier life came intellectual traits of profound importance. The works of travelers along each frontier from colonial days onward describe certain common traits, and these traits have, while softening down, still persisted as survivals in the place of their origin, even when a higher social organization succeeded. The result is that to the frontier the American intellect owes its striking characteristics. That coarseness and strength combined with acuteness and inquisitiveness; that practical, inventive turn of mind, quick to find expedients; that masterful grasp of material things, lacking in the artistic but powerful to effect great ends; that restless, nervous energy;[54] that dominant individualism, working for good and for evil, and withal that buoyancy and exuberance which comes with freedom — these are traits of the frontier, or traits called out elsewhere because of the existence of the frontier. Since the days when the fleet of Columbus sailed into the waters of the New World, America has been another name for opportunity, and the people of the United States have taken their tone from the incessant expansion which has not only been open but has even been forced upon them. He would be a rash prophet who should assert that the expansive character of American life has now entirely ceased. Movement has been its dominant fact, and, unless this training has no effect upon a people, the American energy will continually demand a wider field for its exercise. But never again will such gifts of free land offer themselves. For a moment, at the frontier, the bonds of custom are broken and unrestraint is triumphant. There is not *tabula rasa*. The stubborn American environment is there with its imperious summons to accept its conditions; the inherited ways of doing things are also there; and yet, in spite of environment, and in spite of custom, each frontier did indeed furnish a new field of opportunity, a gate of escape from the bondage of the past; and freshness, and confidence, and scorn of older society, impatience of its restraints and its ideas, and indifference to its lessons, have accompanied the frontier. What the Mediterranean Sea was to the Greeks, breaking the bond of custom, offering new experiences, calling out new institutions and activities, that, and more, the ever retreating frontier has been to the United States directly, and to the nations of Europe more remotely. And now, four centuries from the discovery of America, at the end of a hundred years of life under the Constitution, the frontier has gone, and with its going has closed the first period of American history.

Notes

1. Since the meeting of the American Historical Association, this paper has also been given as an address to the State Historical Society of Wisconsin, December 14, 1893. I have to thank the Secretary of the Society, Mr. Reuben G. Thwaites, for securing valuable material for my use in the preparation of the paper.

2. Abridgment of Debates of Congress, V, p. 706.

3. Bancroft (1860 ed.), III, pp. 344, 345, citing Logan MSS.; [Mitchell] Contest in America, etc. (1752), p. 237.

4. Kercheval, History of the Valley; Bernheim, German Settlements in the Carolinas; Winsor, Narrative and Critical History of America, V, p. 304; Colonial Records

of North Carolina, IV, p. xx; Weston, Documents Connected with the History of South Carolina, p. 82; Ellis and Evans, History of Lancaster County, Pa., chs. III, XXVI.

5. Parkman, Pontiac, II; Griffis, Sir William Johnson, p. 6; Simms's Frontiersmen of New York.

6. Monette, Mississippi Valley, I, p. 311.

7. Wis. Hist. Cols., XI, p. 50; Hinsdale, Old Northwest, p. 121; Burke, "Oration on Conciliation," Works (1872 ed.), I, p. 473.

8. Roosevelt, Winning of the West, and citations there given; Cutler's Life of Cutler.

9. Scribner's Statistical Atlas, xxxviii, pl. 13; McMaster, Hist. of People of U.S., I, pp. 4, 60, 61; Imlay and Filson, Western Territory of America (London, 1793); Rochefoucault-Liancourt, Travels Through the United States of North America (London, 1799); Michaux's "Journal," in Proceedings American Philosophical Society, XXVI, No. 129; Forman, Narrative of a Journey Down the Ohio and Mississippi in 1780–'90 (Cincinnati, 1888); Bartram, Travels Through North Carolina, etc. (London, 1792); Pope, Tour Through the Southern and Western Territories, etc. (Richmond, 1792); Weld, Travels Through the States of North America (London, 1799); Baily, Journal of a Tour in the Unsettled States of North America, 1796–'97 (London, 1856); Pennsylvania Magazine of History, July, 1886; Winsor, Narrative and Critical History of America, VII, pp. 491, 492, citations.

10. Scribner's Statistical Atlas, xxxix.

11. Turner, Character and Influence of the Indian Trade in Wisconsin (Johns Hopkins University Studies, Series IX), pp. 61 ff.

12. Monette, History of the Mississippi Valley, II; Flint, Travels and Residence in Mississippi; Flint, Geography and History of the Western States; Abridgment of Debates of Congress, VII, pp. 397, 398, 404; Holmes, Account of the U.S.; Kingdom, America and the British Colonies (London, 1820); Grund, Americans, II, chs. i, iii, vi (although writing in 1836, he treats of conditions that grew out of western advance from the era of 1820 to that time); Peck, Guide for Emigrants (Boston, 1831); Darby, Emigrants' Guide to Western and Southwestern States and Territories; Dana, Geographical Sketches in the Western Country; Kinzie, Waubun; Keating, Narrative of Long's Expedition; Schoolcraft, Discovery of the Sources of the Mississippi River, Travels in the Central Portions of the Mississippi Valley, and Lead Mines of the Missouri; Andreas, History of Illinois, I, 86–99; Hurlbut, Chicago Antiquities; McKenney, Tour to the Lakes; Thomas, Travels through the Western Country, etc. (Auburn, N.Y., 1819).

13. Darby, Emigrants' Guide, pp. 272 ff.; Benton, Abridgment of Debates, VII, p. 397.

14. DeBow's Review, IV, p. 254; XVII, p. 428.

15. Grund, Americans, II, p. 8.

16. Peck, New Guide to the West (Cincinnati, 1848), ch. IV; Parkman, Oregon Trail; Hall, The West (Cincinnati, 1848); Pierce, Incidents of Western Travel; Murray, Travels in North America; Lloyd, Steamboat Directory (Cincinnati, 1856); "Forty Days in a Western Hotel" (Chicago), in Putnam's Magazine, December 1894; Mackay, The Western World, II, ch. II, III; Meeker, Life in the West; Bogen, German in America (Boston, 1851); Olmstead, Texas Journey; Greeley, Recollections of a Busy Life; Schouler, History of the United States, V, 261–67; Peyton, Over the Alleghanies and Across the Prairies (London, 1870); Loughborough, The Pacific Telegraph and Railway (St. Louis, 1849); Whitney, Project for a Railroad to the Pacific (New York, 1849);

Peyton, Suggestions on Railroad Communication with the Pacific, and the Trade of China and the Indian Islands; Benton, Highway to the Pacific (a speech delivered in the U.S. Senate, December 16, 1850).

17. A writer in The Home Missionary (1850), p. 239, reporting Wisconsin conditions, exclaims: "Think of this, people of the enlightened East. What an example, to come from the very frontiers of civilization!" But one of the missionaries writes: "In a few years Wisconsin will no longer be considered as the West, or as an outpost of civilization, any more than western New York, or the Western Reserve."

18. Bancroft (H. H.), History of California, History of Oregon, and Popular Tribunals; Shinn, Mining Camps.

19. See the suggestive paper by Prof. Jesse Macy, The Institutional Beginnings of a Western State.

20. Shinn, Mining Camps.

21. Compare Thorpe, in Annals American Academy of Political and Social Science, September, 1891; Bryce, American Commonwealth (1888), II, p. 689.

22. Loria, Analisi della Proprieta Capitalista, II, p. 15.

23. Compare Observations on the North American Land Company, London, 1796, pp. xv, 144; Logan, History of Upper South Carolina, I, pp. 149–51; Turner, Character and Influence of Indian Trade in Wisconsin, p. 18; Peck, New Guide for Emigrants (Boston, 1837), ch. IV; Compendium Eleventh Census, I, p. xl.

24. See pages 220, 221, 223, post, for illustrations of the political accompaniments of changed industrial conditions.

25. But Lewis and Clark were the first to explore the route from the Missouri to the Columbia.

26. Narrative and Critical History of America, VIII, p. 10; Sparks' Washington Works, IX, pp. 303, 327; Logan, History of Upper South Carolina, I; McDonald, Life of Kenton, p. 72; Cong. Record. XXIII, p. 57.

27. On the effect of the fur trade in opening the routes of migration, see the author's Character and Influence of the Indian Trade in Wisconsin.

28. Lodge, English Colonies, p. 152 and citations; Logan, Hist. of Upper South Carolina, I, p. 151.

29. Flint, Recollections, p. 9.

30. See Monette, Mississippi Valley, I, p. 344.

31. Coues' Lewis and Clark's Expedition, I, pp. 2, 253–59; Benton, in Cong. Record, XXIII, p. 57.

32. Hehn, Das Salz (Berlin, 1873).

33. Col. Records of N.C., V, p. 3.

34. Findley, History of the Insurrection in the Four Western Counties of Pennsylvania in the Year 1794 (Philadelphia, 1796), p. 35.

35. Hale, Daniel Boone (pamphlet).

36. Compare Baily, Tour in the Unsettled Parts of North America (London, 1856), pp. 217–19, where a similar analysis is made for 1796. See also Collot, Journey in North America (Paris, 1826), p. 109; Observations on the North American Land Company (London, 1796), pp. xv, 144; Logan, History of Upper South Carolina.

37. "Spotswood Papers," in Collections of Virginia Historical Society, I, II.

38. [Burke], European Settlements, etc. (1765 ed.), II, p. 200.

39. Everest, in Wisconsin Historical Collections, XII, pp. 7 ff.

40. Weston, Documents connected with History of South Carolina, p. 61.

41. See, for example, the speech of Clay, in the House of Representatives, January 30, 1824.

42. See the admirable monograph by Prof. H. B. Adams, Maryland's Influence on the Land Cessions; and also President Welling, in Papers American Historical Association, III, p. 411.

43. Adams Memoirs, IX, pp. 247, 248.

44. Author's article in The Ægis (Madison, Wis.), November 4, 1892.

45. Compare Roosevelt, Thomas Benton, ch. I.

46. Political Science Quarterly, II, p. 457. Compare Sumner, Alexander Hamilton, chs. II–VII.

47. Compare Wilson, Division and Reunion, pp. 15, 24.

48. On the relation of frontier conditions to Revolutionary taxation, see Sumner, Alexander Hamilton, ch. III.

49. I have refrained from dwelling on the lawless characteristics of the frontier, because they are sufficiently well known. The gambler and desperado, the regulators of the Carolinas and the vigilantes of California, are types of that line of scum that the waves of advancing civilization bore before them, and of the growth of spontaneous organs of authority where legal authority was absent. Compare Barrows, United States of Yesterday and To-morrow; Shinn, Mining Camps; and Bancroft, Popular Tribunals. The humor, bravery, and rude strength, as well as the vices of the frontier in its worst aspect, have left traces on American character, language, and literature, not soon to be effaced.

50. Debates in the Constitutional Convention, 1829–1830.

51. [McCrady] Eminent and Representative Men of the Carolinas, I, p. 43; Calhoun's Works, I, pp. 401–06.

52. Speech in the Senate, March 1, 1825; Register of Debates, I, 721.

53. Plea for the West (Cincinnati, 1835), pp. 11 ff.

54. Colonial travelers agree in remarking on the phlegmatic characteristics of the colonists. It has frequently been asked how such a people could have developed that strained nervous energy now characteristic of them. Compare Sumner, Alexander Hamilton, p. 98, and Adams's History of the United States, I, p. 60; IX, pp. 240, 241. The transition appears to become marked at the close of the war of 1812, a period when interest centered upon the development of the West, and the West was noted for restless energy. Grund, Americans, II, ch. I.

Richard White

*When Frederick Jackson Turner and
Buffalo Bill Cody Both Played
Chicago in 1893*

A professor of history at Stanford University, Richard White
is one of the most distinguished and prolific of all western
historians. In this essay, White provocatively compares and
contrasts two giants of western interpretation, Frederick
Jackson Turner and William F. "Buffalo Bill" Cody. Together,
says White, these two storytellers provided overlapping and
yet alternative narratives of the American frontier.

For White, Turner and Buffalo Bill were geniuses in evok-
ing a picture of the frontier. A skilled wordsmith and poet,
Turner portrayed the frontier as a receding wilderness being
"civilized" by advancing farmers. Cody, meanwhile, dramatized the contacts and conflicts between whites and Indians
in his enormously popular Wild West arena exhibition. Both
men popularized the closing frontier and thus dramatized
what they considered one of the great and singular experiences of American — even world — history.

Most of all, White argues, we need to understand both stories. Turner's agricultural frontier and Cody's Wild West are
part of our past. They are, as White concludes, "stories that
define what being an American means." They provide linked
and yet divergent accounts of the frontier, which Turner
and Cody considered the key ingredient to explaining an
exceptional America.

Questions for a Closer Reading

1. According to Richard White, about which parts of the frontier heritage did Turner and Buffalo Bill agree? Disagree?

2. Do you think White has fairly summed up Turner's essay on the significance of the frontier? Why or why not?

3. What are the major ingredients in Buffalo Bill's interpretation of the frontier?

4. In the closing sentence of his essay White says that Turner presented "a coherent and all-encompassing narrative and explanation of the American experience." Try to summarize that narrative in one or two sentences.

5. Iconography, or visual illustration by images and representations, is an important topic in White's essay. What are the images he associates with Buffalo Bill? with Frederick Jackson Turner? Which of these images do you find the most persuasive? Why?

When Frederick Jackson Turner and Buffalo Bill Cody Both Played Chicago in 1893

Americans have never been a people with much use for history, but we do like anniversaries. Frederick Jackson Turner was in Chicago in 1893 as an historian presenting an academic paper on the occasion of the 400th anniversary of Columbus's arrival in the Western Hemisphere. The occasion for this essay is the anniversary of Turner's paper.

Richard White, "When Frederick Jackson Turner and Buffalo Bill Cody Both Played Chicago in 1893," in *Frontier and Region: Essays in Honor of Martin Ridge,* ed. Robert C. Ritchie and Paul Andrew Hutton (San Marino, Calif.: Huntington Library Press; Albuquerque: University of New Mexico Press, 1997), 201–12.

Although they often have educational pretensions, public anniversaries, unlike academic anniversaries, are primarily popular entertainments; and it is the combination of the popular and the educational that makes the figurative meeting of Buffalo Bill Cody and Turner at the Columbian Exposition in Chicago in 1893 so suggestive. Turner was in Chicago, of course, to give an academic talk on the frontier. Buffalo Bill and his Wild West were in Chicago to play twice a day, "every day, rain or shine" at "63rd St — Opposite the World's Fair" before a covered grandstand that could hold 18,000 people.[1] Turner was an educator, an academic, but he had great popular success which arose from his mastery of a popular iconography of the frontier. Buffalo Bill was a showman, but he never referred to his Wild West as a show. His program in 1893 bore the title Buffalo Bill's Wild West and Congress of Rough Riders of the World.[2] Cody had educational pretensions. In one of the innumerable endorsements reproduced in the program, Brick Pomeroy proclaimed the exhibition a "Wild West Reality . . . a correct representation of life on the plains . . . brought to the East for the inspection and education of the public."[3]

The convergence of Buffalo Bill and Turner on Chicago was a happy coincidence for academics like me, but the juxtaposition of Turner and Buffalo Bill is, as Richard Slotkin has fruitfully demonstrated in his *Gunfighter Nation,* a useful and revealing one.[4] I will juxtapose Turner and Buffalo Bill for somewhat different reasons than Slotkin, but, like him, I will take Buffalo Bill Cody as seriously as Frederick Jackson Turner because Cody produced a master narrative of the West as finished and culturally significant as Turner's own.

Turner and Buffalo Bill told separate stories; indeed, each contradicted the other in significant ways. Turner's history was a story of free land, the essentially peaceful occupation of a largely empty continent, and the creation of a unique American identity.[5] The Wild West told a story of violent conquest, of the wresting of the continent from the hands of the American Indian peoples who held it already. Buffalo Bill's story was a fiction, but it was a performance that claimed to represent a history, for, like Turner, Buffalo Bill worked with real historical events and real historical figures.

These different stories demanded different lead characters. For Turner the pioneer was the farmer; for Buffalo Bill the pioneer was the scout. Farmers were peaceful; their conquest was the wilderness. Indians were largely irrelevant to Turner's story, and he never bothered much with them. The scout, however, was the man distinguished by his "knowledge of Indians habits and language, familiar with the hunt, and trustworthy in the hour of extremest danger."[6] He was, as Richard Slotkin has emphasized, the "man who knew Indians" and who ultimately defeated them.[7] In Turner's telling the ax and the plow were the tools of civilization; for Buffalo Bill civilization's tools were the rifle and the bullet. The bullet, the Wild West program declared, is "the pioneer of civilization."[8]

Yet, as different as these narratives were, each drew remarkably similar conclusions from their stories. Both declared the frontier over. Turner built his talk upon "the closing of a great historic movement."[9] Buffalo Bill's 1893 program opened with a conventional enough account of the "rapidly extending frontier" and the West as a scene of "wilderness." But the opening paragraph of the program closes with a significant parenthetical addition: "This last, while perfectly true when written (1883), is at present inapplicable, so fast does law and order progress and pervade the Great West."[10] The frontier, which according to Buffalo Bill, had opened on the Hudson, had now closed. Indeed, Buffalo Bill the Indian fighter and rancher had become Buffalo Bill the promoter of irrigated farming.

Both Turner and Buffalo Bill credited the pioneers with creating a new and distinctive nation, and both worried about what the end of the frontier signified. Buffalo Bill reminded his audience that generations were settling down to enjoy "the homes their fathers located and fenced for them."[11] But by implication the children of the pioneers had disdained, in his program's metaphor, to crowd into cities to live like worms. But with the West won, with free land gone, urban wormdom seemed the inevitable destiny of most Americans.

The major elements of these two very different stories were not new in 1893. Take, for example, the close of the frontier. Predictions of the frontier's imminent demise had been current for a quarter of a century. In 1869 Albert Richardson was already predicting the end of an era in his popular *Beyond the Mississippi*.

> Twenty years ago, half our continent was an unknown land, and the Rocky Mountains were our Pillars of Hercules. Five years hence, the Orient will be our next door neighbor. We shall hold the world's granary, the world's treasury, the world's highway. But we shall have no West, no border, no Civilization, in line of battle, pressing back hostile savages, and conquering hostile nature.[12]

Theodore Roosevelt, wrong about so many things, was correct enough when he credited Turner with having "put into shape a good deal of thought that has been floating around rather loosely." For years now historians have found elements of the Turner thesis presaged in one form or another in the scholarship of the late nineteenth century. Forty years ago Henry Nash Smith took the process one step further by making the Turner thesis itself an expression of the nineteenth-century pastoral myth of the garden.[13]

This contextualization of Turner, and indeed of Buffalo Bill, however, creates a mystery rather than solving one. For if these ideas and symbols were so prevalent, how did the particular versions offered by Turner and Buffalo Bill come to be so culturally dominant and persistent? Why did they over-shadow, and indeed erase, their antecedents and competitors? No one, af-ter all, reads Richardson, and Pawnee Bill — Buffalo Bill's sometime partner and sometimes competitor — is known only to antiquarians.[14]

The answer lies in two things. First, the very contradictions between Turn-er's story and Buffalo Bill's create a clue. Turner and Buffalo Bill, in effect, divided up the existing narratives of American frontier mythology. Each erased part of the larger, and more confusing and tangled, cultural story in order to deliver up a clean, dramatic, and compelling narrative. Richardson, for example, offered a narrative of conquest that emphasized both hostile nature and hostile savages. Turner took as his theme the conquest of nature; he made savagery incidental. Buffalo Bill made the conquest of savages cen-tral; the conquest of nature was incidental. Yet both stories, it must be re-membered, taught the same lessons. Secondly, it was the very ubiquity of the icons of the frontier that allowed both Turner and Buffalo Bill to deliver powerful messages with incredible economy and resonance. Precisely be-cause they could mobilize familiar symbols, Buffalo Bill in a performance of several hours and Frederick Jackson Turner in a short essay could persuade and convince their audiences.

Both Buffalo Bill and Turner were geniuses in their use of the icon-ography of the frontier — but not just with existing stories. The two men also used all kinds of symbolic representations — from log cabins to stage coaches — that were reproduced over and over in American life, then and now. Turner incorporated such icons into his talk. Buffalo Bill set out to rep-resent them. And, indeed, he made himself into a walking icon, at once real and make-believe. As the program put it, "Young, sturdy, a remarkable speci-men of manly beauty, with the brain to conceive and the nerve to execute, Buffalo Bill par excellence is the exemplar of the strong and unique traits that characterize a true American frontiersman."[15] Turner and Buffalo Bill thrived on the modern talent for the mimetic — our ability to duplicate im-ages and experiences.

Turner's "frontier thesis" soon became almost an incantation repeated in thousands of high school and college classrooms and textbooks: "The exis-tence of an area of free land, its continuous recession, and the advance of American settlement westward explains American development." Turner asserted that American westering produced a series of successive frontiers from the Appalachians to the Pacific; the essence of the frontier thesis lay in his claim that in settling these frontiers migrants had created a distinc-tively American democratic outlook. Americans were practical, egalitarian, and democratic because the successive Wests of this country's formative years had provided the "empty" land on which equality and democracy could flourish as integral aspects of progress. Turner's farmers conquered a wilderness and extended what Thomas Jefferson had called an empire of liberty.[16]

Turner summoned the frontier from the dim academic backcountry, but in popular American culture the frontier was already central. Turner did not have to tell Americans about the frontier; he could play off of images they already knew. Ubiquitous representations of covered wagons and log cabins already contained latent narratives of expansion and progress. Americans had already long recognized the cultural utility of the frontier in their politics, folklore, music, literature, art, and speech for generations. All Turner had to do was to tell Americans about the *significance* of this familiar frontier.

Turner masterfully deployed the images of log cabins, wagon trains, and frontier farm making — and the stories that went with them. He made them elements in a sweeping explanation of the nation's past. To the familiar representations of people conquering a "wilderness" and remaking the land, Turner added another dimension. In the process of advancing the frontier, a diverse people of European origins had remade themselves into Americans. He extended the story of progress.[17]

Neither in a spoken paper nor in an academic article could Turner actually use images. Instead, he relied on an almost painterly prose which called to mind familiar images of migration, primitive beginnings, and ultimate progress. Americans already thought in terms of great achievements from primitive beginnings. Americans already thought of themselves as egalitarian and democratic. Americans had already symbolized such beliefs in images of log cabins and migration into a land of opportunity and had turned those images into icons. Turner used the icons.

Turner often placed himself and his audience not in the West but in popular representations of the West. Turner, for instance, instructed his audience to "stand at Cumberland Gap and watch the procession of civilization, marching single file — the buffalo following the trail to the salt springs, the Indian, the fur-trader and hunter, the cattle-raiser, the pioneer farmer — and the frontier has passed by." He asked them to stand figuratively at the same place where George Caleb Bingham had placed the viewer in his "Daniel Boone Escorting Settlers through Cumberland Gap."[18] This standing at the gap, or on the height, or the border, and watching progress unfold was one of the central American icons of the frontier and progress. Turner's prose called to mind countless representations, from the famous and familiar Currier and Ives print, "Across the Continent: Westward the Course of Empire Takes Its Way," to such local variants as "Pictorial Map

Showing the Route Travelled by Mormon Pioneers" (1890). All of them resonated with the Turnerian plot.

Let me take two other examples of the iconography upon which Turner relied: first, in his portrayal of a largely empty continent and, second, in his claim that in America progress involved a regenerative retreat back to the primitive and a recapitulation of ensuing states of civilization.[19] Iconographic representations of both ideas were ubiquitous in American life.

The portrayal of North America as largely empty and unknown was a cartographic convention by the nineteenth century, but this had not always been so. Earlier maps of the sixteenth and seventeenth centuries, for example, had portrayed a densely occupied continent teeming with people. Europeans knew little of the interior, but they assumed that it was fully occupied. But by the nineteenth century, all this had changed. In illustrated maps, as in contemporary prints, only a few scattered Indians appear. They were either retreating or quietly observing the coming of whites. The maps Americans saw in schools broadcast the same message even more forcefully. Emma Willard's widely used nineteenth-century school text vividly portrays the West as empty land. Small villages of French Canadians appear on the map, but Willard has completely erased Indians. This message of a largely empty continent peacefully occupied recurred in the popular literature of the West. Joaquin Miller's "Westward Ho," for example, celebrated a conquest without the guilt of "studied battle":

> O bearded, stalwart, westmost men,
> So tower-like, so Gothic built
> A kingdom won without the guilt
> Of studied battle, that hath been
> Your blood's inheritance . . .

Turner recognized conflict with the Indians, but it was merely part of a much larger contact with wilderness that necessitated the pioneers' initial regression and subsequent recapitulation of the stages of civilization. The "wilderness," Turner declared in Chicago, "masters the colonist . . . it puts him in the log cabin of the Cherokee and Iroquois . . ."[20] This association of pioneers with Indians through the log cabin is interesting, for by the 1890s the log cabin had long been the chief icon of the nineteenth-century frontier. Indeed, the log cabin was perhaps the central American icon. A cabin, built with simple tools and from local materials, proclaimed self-reliance and a connection with place. Usually isolated, it stressed the courage of the builder and the challenge that the surrounding wilderness represented. But, most of all and most interestingly, the cabin had come to represent progress.

The cabin was not intrinsically a representation of progress. Indeed, one of the earliest and most beautiful and haunting representations of the log cabin, the etching in the atlas accompanying Collot's *Voyage dans L'Amerique Septentronale*, stressed only the isolation and the primitiveness of the structure. Similarly, at midcentury George Caleb Bingham's printing of a squatter's cabin had little progressive about it.[21] And later, in different contexts, sharecroppers' cabins or cabins in Appalachia represented backwardness and poverty rather than progress and prosperity. Only when coupled with the knowledge of the success that was to follow did the cabin proclaim great achievements from small beginnings. Presidential births in supposed log cabins took on meaning only in light of the subsequent presidency. Lincoln's cabin took on meaning with the knowledge of Lincoln's later achievements.[22] The achievements of modern America gave progressive meaning to frontier cabins. The cabin demanded such pairings to evoke its national historical narrative of progress achieved through self-reliance and energy.

The iconography of the cabin served in a quite real way as a groundwork for Turner. The cabin icon already associated the frontier with a retreat to the primitive followed by progress to great achievements. It had served as a symbol of personal and political progress in William Henry Harrison's Log Cabin campaign and in the Lincoln campaign. It was prominently featured in contemporary sheet music and local and popular histories.

But the cabin iconography probably most clearly prefigured Turner in the county histories and atlases that proliferated throughout the Midwest in the 1880s. A common feature in these books were illustrations of prosperous contemporary farms that included, either somewhere in the picture itself or as an inset, a log cabin. The movement from the cabin to the developed farm signified progress. Early maps of Chicago employed the same imagery. The Turner thesis was infinitely more sophisticated than either the county histories or popular histories, but each developed the same theme. These works had, in effect, prepared the way for Turner. His work would resonate with its readers, giving sophisticated form to what they already knew and accepted.

In 1893 Buffalo Bill told another story and employed a different set of icons. Perhaps the easiest way to see how his story differed from that of Turner is to look at the role Indians played in each. Indians were not so much absent from Turner as peripheral; they were not intrinsic to the meaning of his narrative. But Indians were everywhere in Buffalo Bill's Wild West. An Indian illustrated the advertisement in the *Chicago Tribune*. Illustrations of Indians were prominent throughout the program. A "horde of war-painted Arapahos, Cheyenne, and Sioux Indians" participated in the Wild West.[23]

The role of these Indians in the show was to attack. Many of the great set pieces of the Wild West—an attack on the "Prairie Emigrant Train Crossing the Plains," the "Capture of the Deadwood Mail Coach by the Indians," and, most famous of all, "The Battle of the Little Big Horn, Showing with Historical Accuracy the Scene of Custer's Last Charge"—featured Indian attacks.[24]

Buffalo Bill offered what to a modern historian seems an odd story of conquest, for it is an account of Indian aggression and white defense, of Indian killers and white victims, of, in effect, badly abused conquerors. These reenactments open a window onto a particularly interesting aspect of the American iconography of the frontier. To achieve Joaquin Miller's "kingdom won without the guilt of studied battle," Americans had to create an iconography that turned conquerors into victims. The great military icons of American westward expansion are not victories, they are defeats: the Alamo and the Battle of the Little Big Horn. We do not plan our conquests. We just retaliate against massacres.

Like Turner, Buffalo Bill found both the theme and the icons for this version of conquest readily available. The theme of white victimization was so common that Turner himself, in what amounted to an aside, similarly made conquerors into victims. He spoke of Indians as a "common danger" which kept alive "the power of resistance to aggression." He, as much as Buffalo Bill, presented this striking historical reversal of the actual situation as mere conventional wisdom.[25] What gave this reversal of roles its power was a popular iconography that surrounded Americans with images of valiant white victims overpowered by numerous savage assailants. In the version of the frontier Buffalo Bill developed, the continent was no longer empty; it teemed with murderous Indian enemies.

Buffalo Bill exploited an iconography that stretched back to Puritan captivity narratives and continued through the wars of the eighteenth and early nineteenth century. Nineteenth-century broadsides such as the "Massacre of Baldwin's Family by Savages" and "Murder of the whole family of Samuel Wells . . . by the Indians" kept this theme of white victimization central to American understanding of the Indian wars.

Buffalo Bill played no small part in making the defeat of Custer and the slaughter of most of his command both the culmination and the chief icon of this version of conquest. Where representation stopped and lived experience began were never very clear in Buffalo Bill's Wild West, and this gave the Wild West its power. Buffalo Bill created what now seems a postmodern West, in which performance and history were hopelessly intertwined. The story Buffalo Bill told gained credence from his claim (and the claim of many of the Indians who accompanied him) that he had lived part of it.

The show and lived historical reality constantly imitated each other. Sitting Bull, whom Americans credited with being the architect of Custer's defeat, had toured with the Wild West. Some of the Sioux who charged Custer at the Little Big Horn would later charge him nightly in the Wild West. And Indians who fought whites in the Wild West would return to the Dakotas to fight whites for real during the Ghost Dance* troubles. Buffalo Bill would step off the stage during both the Custer campaign and during the Ghost Dance to serve as an army scout, each time incorporating aspects of his experience into the show.

The most dramatic and revealing example of this complicated mimesis is the Yellow Hand incident. Leaving the stage in Wilmington, Delaware, in June 1876, Buffalo Bill had joined the Fifth Cavalry as a scout. He was in the field when the Sioux defeated Custer. During a skirmish that July he had killed and scalped a Cheyenne named Yellow Hand.[26] The skirmish and Yellow Hand were being assimilated into Buffalo Bill's stage persona even as it happened. Buffalo Bill had prepared for the anticipated engagement by dressing in his showman's outfit — "a Mexican vaquero outfit of black velvet slashed with scarlet and trimmed with silver buttons and lace" — which then could become in his performances the actual clothing in which he fought Yellow Hand.[27] Yellow Hand became the "first scalp for Custer." And the scalp, on display in theaters where Buffalo Bill performed in the "realistic Western Drama, . . . Life on the Border" became an actual prop in Buffalo Bill's performances that year.[28]

Joining Buffalo Bill in these pre–Wild West performances in 1877 was Captain Jack Crawford, the Poet Scout. Captain Jack went on to a long career of his own, but Custer and Buffalo Bill gave him his big break. Jack Crawford was an Omaha janitor who, traveling west to enlist with Custer (or so he said), got early news of the defeat and had the presence of mind to telegraph the story to the New York papers. He adopted the persona of a frontier scout who had carried the news from the battlefield and then appears to have been able to turn that fabricated experience as a scout into some real, but brief, army experience in the Southwest.

These combinations of experience and representation were quite malleable. In 1877 Buffalo Bill and Captain Jack, while performing together, combined their stories into a new one in which Buffalo Bill sent a dispatch to Captain Jack on Custer's death. This had supposedly been the occasion for Captain Jack to write a rather confused poem, "Custer's Death," which Buffalo Bill reproduced in the program for "Life on the Border." The poem demanded vengeance from "these demons" who killed Custer. The vic-

---

Ghost Dance: The Ghost Dances were part of an important religious and revitalization movement among Native Americans during the late nineteenth century. One leader of the movement, Wovoka (c. 1856–1932), preached that if Indians danced and followed ceremonial rituals, they would be reunited with deceased relatives and friends, be regenerated culturally, and be protected from the weapons of frontier soldiers.

timized Custer was to be avenged by volunteers whose identity (much like Captain Jack's own) wavered from stanza to stanza. Their efforts would not "leave a red."

As bewildering as the details of the anticipated slaughter of the Indians might be, the basic message was clear. The slaughter of the heroic Custer justified retaliatory massacre and revenge.[29] The inversion of aggressor and victim justified conquest, and it was played out over and over again.

Turner's "Significance of the Frontier" and Buffalo Bill's Wild West stand in complicated and revealing relation to each other. It is a point that we miss by trivializing Buffalo Bill and missing the common grounding of his story and that of Turner. To see Turner as serious and significant and Buffalo Bill as a charlatan and a curiosity, to see Turner as history and Buffalo Bill as entertainment, to see one as concerned with reality and the other with myth, misses their common reliance and promotion of the iconography of their time; it misses their ability to follow separate, but connected, strands of a single mythic cloth. And it misses, too, the ways in which, just as in Chicago in 1893, these seemingly contradictory stories only ultimately make historical sense when told simultaneously.

These are still essential stories because they are stories that define what being an American means. We still tell variants of both stories. And, indeed, for all the variant multicultural histories that the new western history introduces, these new histories will exist largely within the plotlines of these stories of conquest and stories of peaceful progress.

Indeed, the city of Chicago, where both Buffalo Bill Cody presented his Wild West and Frederick Jackson Turner delivered his paper in 1893, frequently represented itself in strikingly Turnerian terms of primitive beginnings, progress, and opportunity. Turner, in effect, wrote off of these icons; he made them part of a coherent and all-encompassing narrative and explanation of the American experience.

Notes

1. See the advertisement in the *Chicago Tribune,* April 27, 1893.

2. *Buffalo Bill's Wild West and Congress of Rough Riders of the World* (Chicago: Blakely Printing Company, 1893), title page. The standard biography of Buffalo Bill is Don Russell, *The Lives and Legends of Buffalo Bill* (Norman: University of Oklahoma Press, 1960). Russell has also written the most comprehensive study of Wild West shows; see his *The Wild West or, A History of the Wild West Shows* (Fort Worth, Tex.: Amon Carter Museum of Western Art, 1970).

3. *Buffalo Bill's Wild West,* 9.

4. Richard Slotkin, *Gunfighter Nation: The Myth of the Frontier in Twentieth-Century America* (New York: Atheneum, 1992).

5. Frederick Jackson Turner, *The Significance of the Frontier in American History*

(New York: Frederick Ungar, 1975). Turner did not entirely ignore Indians; he wrote, for example, that each frontier "was won by a series of Indian wars" (p. 33). He did, however, marginalize them: the *frontier,* defined as land populated by two people or more per square mile, did not, for example, include Indians (p. 29). Turner associated Indians with French traders not English farmers (pp. 36–37). Elements of Buffalo Bill's story were present in Turner's narrative — Indians were important for presenting "a common danger," necessitating rugged frontiersmen who would "resist aggression" (p. 38) — but these elements were a minor part of Turner's story.

6. *Buffalo Bill's Wild West,* 4.

7. Slotkin, *Gunfighter Nation.*

8. *Buffalo Bill's Wild West,* 22.

9. Turner, *The Significance of the Frontier,* 27.

10. *Buffalo Bill's Wild West,* 4.

11. *Buffalo Bill's Wild West,* 10.

12. Albert Richardson, *Beyond the Mississippi* (Hartford: American Publishing Company, 1867), i. Proclamations of the centrality of the frontier were a staple of mid- and late-nineteenth-century writing: Justin Winsor, *Narrative and Critical History of America,* vol. 8 (New York: Houghton, Mifflin, and Company, 1888), Theodore Roosevelt, *The Winning of the West,* vol. I (New York: G. P. Putnam's Sons, 1889), Henry Howe, *Historical Collections of the Great West* (Cincinnati: H. Howe, 1856).

13. Henry Nash Smith, *Virgin Land: The American West as Symbol and Myth* (Cambridge, Mass.: Harvard University Press, 1970; orig. ed., 1950), 251.

14. For Pawnee Bill and other Wild West shows, see Russell, *The Wild West,* 32–33, 50–52, 75–76, 98–103, 129–33, and passim.

15. *Buffalo Bill's Wild West,* 7.

16. Turner, *The Significance of the Frontier,* 27–28, 51–52, 57. My emphasis here is on Turner's talk in Chicago in 1893. I have given a wider analysis of Turner's historical thinking elsewhere; see Richard White, "Frederick Jackson Turner," in John Wunder, ed., *Historians of the American Frontier: A Bio-Bibliographical Source Book* (Westport, Connecticut: Greenwood Press, 1988), 660–81.

17. Turner, *The Significance of the Frontier,* 44–45.

18. Bingham's painting, as Nancy Rash has emphasized, was notable for the way it featured pioneer families. She details its initial disappointing reception and its reproduction as a mass-produced print. Nancy Rash, *The Painting and Politics of George Caleb Bingham* (New Haven: Yale University Press, 1991), 60–65.

19. Turner, *The Significance of the Frontier,* 28–29.

20. Turner, *The Significance of the Frontier,* 29.

21. For "The Squatters," see Rash, *Painting and Politics,* 58–60.

22. For a comparison of the log cabin mythology and actual social origins of presidents, see Edward Pessen, *The Log Cabin Myth: The Social Backgrounds of the Presidents* (New Haven: Yale University Press, 1984), 10–26.

23. *Chicago Tribune,* April 27, 1893, p. 2.

24. *Buffalo Bill's* Program. See also Russell, *The Wild West,* 27, 46.

25. Turner, *The Significance of the Frontier,* 38.

26. For Yellow Hand, see Russell, *The Lives and Legends of Buffalo Bill,* 219–35, and Paul Andrew Hutton, ed., *Ten Days on the Plains* (Dallas: DeGolyer Library/SMU Press, 1985), 35–41.

27. Russell, *The Lives and Legends of Buffalo Bill,* 231.

28. Buffalo Bill (W. F. Cody) and Captain Jack (J. W. Crawford), "Life on the Border," Program, Oakland, Calif., June 13, 1877, copy in Everett D. Graff Collection of Western Americana, 783, Newberry Library. For an account of the play in the East and the attack on the display of the scalp, see Russell, *The Lives and Legends of Buffalo Bill,* 254–55.

29. Captain Jack Crawford, "Custer's Death," in Buffalo Bill (W. F. Cody) and Captain Jack (J. W. Crawford), "Life on the Border," Program, Oakland, Calif., June 13, 1877, copy in Everett D. Graff Collection of Western Americana, 783, Newberry Library. Also see Darlis A. Miller, *Captain Jack Crawford: Buckskin Poet, Scout, and Showman* (Albuquerque: University of New Mexico Press, 1993).

3. Whose frontier is it?

Glenda Riley

Frederick Jackson Turner Overlooked the Ladies

Glenda Riley, Bracken Professor of History at Ball State University and the country's leading interpreter of women on the frontier and in the American West, argues that Frederick Jackson Turner clearly omitted women from his story of the frontier. In overlooking women's important roles in pioneer history, Riley adds, Turner was ironically exceptionalist, fostering a frontier story devoted entirely to men's actions.

Riley notes four reasons that might explain why Turner overlooked women in writing about the frontier. First, Turner taught history "in a largely male enclave," which effectively insulated him from female colleagues. In addition, he based his work on previous writers who paid scant attention to women's activities. Third, fascinated with political and economic history, Turner did little work in social history. Finally, Turner's emphasis on institutional history and his ties to scientific historical writing prompted him to overlook the roles of dynamic individuals. As Riley points out, "Turner studied masses of people, types rather than individuals." A careful reading of Riley's criticisms of Turner should raise several questions in the minds of readers.

Questions for a Closer Reading

1. How exceptional can the frontier experience be if the roles of women are neither known nor studied?

2. If Turner did not say much about women and minority groups, are his writings so flawed by these omissions that they lack relevance for our time?

3. Do you expect writers of the 1890s to be interested in the same topics that intrigue authors and readers today, a century later?

4. Which of Riley's points do you find the most valid? Why?

5. Which of her points is most helpful in understanding Turner as man and historian?

Frederick Jackson Turner Overlooked the Ladies

Like John Adams during the mid-1770s, Frederick Jackson Turner often failed to "remember the ladies."* Although Turner was an observant and insightful historian, he overlooked the role of women in the United States' westward migration. In his path-breaking essay of 1893, "The Significance of the Frontier in American History," as well as in later articles and books, Turner characterized America's expansionist phase as a male phenomenon.

By ignoring women, Turner helped create a tunnel vision that his followers perpetuated in the area of study he loved — sectionalism and the American West. Instead of enlarging Turner's viewpoint to include such groups as women, they supported and repeated Turner's primary argu-

---

*"*Remember the ladies*": Abigail Adams, wife of Revolutionary leader and later president, John Adams, reminded her husband in March 1776 to "remember the ladies" as he wrote legislation for the new country. She called for protection of her place as a wife and mother, not for tradition-breaking roles for women in the new society.

Glenda Riley, "Frederick Jackson Turner Overlooked the Ladies," *Journal of the Early Republic* 13 (Summer 1993): 216–30.

ments. Eminent historian Carl Becker frequently maintained that the frontier was a process rather than a geographic place, that it inculcated individualism into Americans, and that idealism and freedom ever prevailed within its bounds. Frederic L. Paxson supported the continuing validity of Turner's ideas pretty much as he had originally stated them.[1] Moreover, Turner's ideas encouraged such social commentators as Herbert Croly to conclude that America's "virgin wilderness" made the United States a "Land of Promise," and such novelists as Hamlin Garland to proclaim "a faith in the open spaces." None of these Turnerian commentators considered the effects of wilderness and space on women.[2]

Why Turner ignored women and the results of that omission are seldom explored, but on this, the one-hundredth anniversary of Turner's famous address, both questions deserve examination. If we are to free ourselves totally from this oversight in Turner's thesis, it is necessary to understand his thinking rather than accept superficial explanations for his neglect of women. Probably the most common reason given for Turner's inattention to women is that his omission was typical of his times, that few people were sensitive to women's roles and contributions during the late 1800s and early 1900s. Perhaps John Adams, a man of the late eighteenth century, can be excused on such grounds, but Turner, a man of the late nineteenth and early twentieth centuries, should not get off so easily.

How could a man hailed as an astute observer and critical thinker turn a blind eye to the significant changes women had experienced since John and Abigail Adams's day? Born in 1861 in Portage, Wisconsin, Turner lived during one of the most turbulent eras in American history. In Portage, he participated in the development of a western town, watching as men and women molded their own lives and contributed to the formation of the region and the nation. Between the time Turner left Portage in 1880 to seek a bachelor's degree in Madison and his death in 1932 in Pasadena, California, he came into contact with thousands of students, worked as a journalist, served as a professor at the University of Wisconsin between 1889 and 1910 and at Harvard University between 1910 and 1924, and later as research associate at the Huntington Library.[3] Among numerous other events, during his seventy years Turner lived through the well-publicized rise in numbers of women in paid employment and the professions, the increasing momentum of the woman suffrage movement beginning in 1890 and triumphing in 1920, and the frequent debates regarding what were then known as the "woman question" and the "new" woman.

Moreover, in his personal life Turner spent a great deal of time with women and regarded them with affection and esteem. Turner credited his mother, Mary Hanford Turner, a former schoolteacher, with helping develop his fondness for books and ideas. Later, Turner doted on his wife,

Caroline Mae Sherwood, and their three children. In 1897, for example, Turner inquired about the social possibilities for Mae should he accept an appointment at Princeton University.[4] Turner was a devoted family man, who never fully recovered from the deaths in 1899 of his five-year-old daughter, Mae Sherwood, and his seven-year-old son, Jackson Allen. According to a friend, his children's deaths "tinctured" Turner's life until its end.[5] After this tragedy, Turner increasingly centered his personal life on Mae and the surviving daughter, Dorothy. In 1905, Turner rejected historian Max Farrand's suggestion that he take a leave-of-absence for a month each year to research and write; he feared such a practice would create a "nomadic life" for his family, and he was unwilling to leave them behind. He added that "a man owes something to his family as well as to scholarship."[6]

Not only did Turner include women in virtually all aspects of his personal life, but he welcomed them into his classroom. Just as he sent daughter Dorothy to college he also encouraged women students who sought him out. Louise Phelps Kellogg recalled that she participated in both the first "West" class that Turner offered and his seminar. Like the men in the seminar, she and the one other female student worked in "comradeship" with Turner. In 1938, Kellogg, who for more than forty years served as editor, lecturer, and author at the Wisconsin Historical Society, declared that Turner "had a greater influence in reshaping American historiography than any other of his generation."[7] Turner too had kind words for his women students. He not only expressed pride in Kellogg's achievements, but likewise took credit for training others such as Helen Blair, who in 1911 dedicated to Turner her *Indian Tribes of the Upper Mississippi Valley*.[8]

Turner also counted women among his many friends. In 1908, he regaled Farrand with an account of a month he and his family spent in the Maine woods camping and boating with several other men and women.[9] Then, during his Harvard years, Turner formed a fast friendship with a Bostonian, Alice Forbes Perkins Hooper, a socialite, philanthropist, and suffragist who shared Turner's passion for the American West. Beginning in 1910, Hooper and Turner visited, corresponded, and tried to build a collection of western history source materials at Harvard. As their friendship grew, Hooper began to call Turner "Historicus." In 1915, Hooper wrote to Turner that "you and all you stand for are a great asset in my garden of friends." In 1931, Hooper again mentioned that she regarded their "comfortable" friendship as one of her most important resources. Turner, who addressed Hooper as "Dear Lady," returned her esteem. In 1915, he assured her that, "you are the best thing I have discovered in New England," and in 1930, "How much I value and appreciate you!"[10]

Obviously, Turner was attuned to women and aware of their concerns. Yet he persistently overlooked women, their roles, and their contributions in his scholarship. When Turner did mention women, he portrayed them as simply part of the family unit. As men pushed their families westward, Turner explained, "daughters walked beside the mother, who rode on the horse."[11] And in 1897, Turner noted that while successful western entrepreneurs sought political influence and sent their sons to college, their wives and daughters made "extensive visits to Europe."[12] Nearly all Turner's historical actors were male, wore hunting shirts, brandished weapons, and wielded axes. "Before long," Turner wrote of his male pioneer, "he has gone to planting Indian corn and plowing with a sharp stick; he shouts the war cry and takes the scalp in orthodox Indian fashion."[13]

Reconciling Turner's sensitive and affectionate personal treatment of women with his neglectful and even patronizing treatment of them in his scholarly writing requires more than the lame excuse that few people in Turner's day paid much attention to women. Rather, this essay maintains that Turner neglected women in his scholarship for four major reasons. The easiest to identify is that Turner studied, taught, and made friends in a largely male enclave where his oversight never was challenged.[14] He discussed his ideas with such people as his good friend Woodrow Wilson, who as a political scientist and aspiring politician believed in the evolution of institutions and emphasized the need for strong (male) national leadership to bind together the sections of the United States.[15] Such others as southern historian Ulrich Bonnell Phillips, once a colleague of Turner's at the University of Wisconsin and a lifelong friend, declared that Turner's portraits of frontier society manifested "brilliance in analysis and perfection in phrase." No modifications or additions to Turner's thought seemed necessary to the men of his profession.[16]

A second reason for Turner's dismissal of women was his tendency to draw heavily on earlier writers, all of whom overlooked women. Although his supporters, especially his student Carl Becker, maintained that Turner's thesis was a "novel doctrine," critics have pointed out that Turner borrowed from a number of other writers.[17] Among these was Jean-Jacques Rousseau, who believed that a return to nature would improve society (meaning men); when he commented on women, Rousseau maintained that they existed to serve and care for men. Others included James Fenimore Cooper, who elevated the habits of his pioneer folk-heroes, primarily males, to a historical force and Ralph Waldo Emerson who, as early as 1844, emphasized the West's Americanizing influence in his lecture, "The Young American," also meaning men. After the Civil War, journalist E. L. Godkin also wrote only of men when he pointed to "frontier life" as the distinguishing feature of American society and commented on the frontier's relation to the "democratic tide." So did Italian social philosopher Achille Loria, who developed a "free land" theory of history from whom Turner borrowed a central feature of his frontier thesis.[18] Because Turner knew of the work of these men as well as of Francis Parkman and Theodore Roosevelt, his emphasis on the West was far from unique; indeed, the West had been a symbol of American thought, and of American nationalism, since the early nineteenth century.[19]

Turner's reliance on earlier views of the American West naturally led him to adopt traditional ideas regarding women. By borrowing from writers ranging from Rousseau to Loria, Turner absorbed social constructs that not only subsumed women under the generic category "men," but also viewed women as non-actors. Therefore, although Turner argued that historians should view the past through present concerns, the contemporary significance of such issues as women's rights and roles escaped him.[20] At least partly because he absorbed older interpretations of women as passive beings who were secondary in the overall scheme, he selected nationalism and American character, meaning male character, as the dominant issues through which to view the past.

Already at a disadvantage regarding the importance of women in history, Turner suffered a third limitation: a decided fascination with political and economic explanations. Although Turner claimed that his experience as a journalist, especially the years he spent under the tutelage of his editor father, Andrew Jackson Turner, gave him a sense of reality and forced him to see "the connections of many factors with the purely political," he in fact developed a political view of history.[21] According to Martin Ridge, "Turner expressed himself with the imagery of a poet and speculated about the past with the language of a seer" yet "at heart . . . believed in economic and political history."[22]

After all, Turner did his Ph.D. work in international law, principles of economics, church history, and the history of politics and economic thought. He taught political and constitutional history at Madison. In 1891 he announced a new course titled "Economic and Social [meaning social forces rather than groups of people] History of the United States."[23] Finally, Turner's mentor, Professor William Francis Allen, had studied the Roman empire from the standpoint of its economic expansion and political institutions. Clearly, few influences in his training or professional life pushed Turner toward a scholarly consideration of women or any other specific social group. Instead, when innovative impulses struck, Turner suggested as additional research topics agriculture, public lands, and urban development.[24]

Finally, Turner considered himself a scientific historian who sought knowledge of causal dynamics and larger explanations rather than the deeds and achievements of individuals or of such groups of people as women.[25] Unlike gifted "lay" historians such as Francis Parkman, Theodore Roosevelt, and James Ford Rhodes, who emphasized individual agency and specific episodes, Turner and his graduate-school-trained colleagues focused upon processes. As early as 1887–1888, while still working on his master's degree, Turner wrote that he preferred to deal with historical materials from a "genetic standpoint," pursuing over-arching topics rather than individuals or types of people.[26]

Turner hoped to identify the origins of institutions, or what he called the "social foundations" of American history, while avoiding chronology, narrative, and even specific institutional studies. As one of his admirers noted, Turner was an "interpreter" and thus always "impatient of narrative for its own sake,"[27] In his search for wider contexts, for organizing principles, for the universal rather than the particular, Turner studied masses of people, types rather than individuals, *the* people rather than people themselves.

As his thought developed, Turner thus defined frontier in a way that made it a series of processes. In 1896, for example, Turner described the West as a "form" of society and a "constructive force" rather than a geographic area.[28] In 1906, he wrote of "institutions," "conditions," and "interests."[29] Two years later, he declared that "the story of individual leaders, and narrative of events sank into insignificance" in the face of the migration of people and development of society.[30] And in 1911, he spoke of "forces," "currents," and "movements."[31]

Turner's own words made clear that his view of history had little room for such specific groups as women. As Carl Becker explained, Turner assumed that "commonplace people, acting in commonplace ways . . . determine the social process." According to Becker, Turner was an expositor who was interested in larger forces than individuals.[32] This approach made people little more than categories—Indians, settlers, immigrants, farmers, or the "hunter type."[33] Women simply inhabited each of the various categories. Therefore, even when Turner studied such rich and revealing sources as census records, rather than seize upon numbers of marriages, children, and gainfully employed females as useful data, he concentrated upon population density and voting statistics.

As a result of these four limiting influences on his thought, Turner became a major myth-maker of the scholarly world.[34] He was aware of some of his biases; in opening lectures he often apologized for the need to make generalizations in the face of conflicting or nonexistent evidence, observers' prejudices, and distorting contemporary values.[35] Still, he failed to note his omission of women and continued to disseminate masculine generalizations regarding the American West. Proudly, Turner passed on a male-dominated West to generations of scholars. One of his favorite boasts was that he had not only originated the course "History of the West," but had trained "a considerable portion" of its instructors.[36]

Turner's narrow perspective helped perpetuate a lack of historical knowledge concerning women in the American West, a vacuum that popular culture happily filled throughout the late nineteenth and early twentieth centuries. Long bereft of guidance from historians, a sizeable number of writers, artists, and performers invented mythologized western women. Because no women existed in the historian's West, shapers of popular culture supplied interpretations that fell into two types: images based upon traditional beliefs regarding American women and those derived from more modern conceptions of women.

On the one hand, writers, artists, and film-makers who resisted changes in women's status usually thought of western women as inferior beings in need of protection. In their view, western women often fell victim to harsh climate, hard work, or the supposed "rape, pillage, and burn" mentality of Native Americans. Dime novels especially portrayed western women as delicate creatures in need of rescue, but thousands of others pursued a similar theme. In 1892, Emeline Fuller's *Left by the Indians,* a saga of torture imposed upon defenseless white women, gained best-seller status.[37] From novelist Hamlin Garland's despondent "Pioneer Mother" to artist W. D. Koerner's woeful "Madonna of the Prairie" to Hollywood's female flowers, popular culture replaced Turner's invisible women with vulnerable ones.

On the other hand, image-makers who supported and even applauded changes in women's status generally promoted active images of western women: the cowgirl, shooter, heroine, and survivor. The very summer that Frederick Jackson Turner delivered his now-famous address on the grounds of the World Fair in Chicago, Buffalo Bill Cody's Wild West played outside its gates. Literally under Turner's nose, Annie Oakley — the archetypal representation of the hardy and competent western woman — performed astounding feats with rifles and pistols, while cowgirls, among others, circled the arena on horseback and thrilled the audience with a variety of stunts. Unlike Turner, Cody realized that women had helped develop the West and he understood that females in his audiences wanted to learn about such women. Thus, Turner's and other historians' default enhanced Cody's opportunity to attract crowds to his particular version of western women.

Writers also supplied the public with strong and daring western women. From Ned Buntline to Prentiss Ingraham, dime novelists increasingly exchanged female victims for heroines. Then, in 1927 social commentator Ellsworth Huntington did what Turner had not done: he connected the West to the superiority of American women. Writing in *The Nation,* Huntington argued that American women were brave, bold, competent, ambitious, and even unique because of the nation's "pioneer period." The frontier had weeded out the weak and had stimulated surviving women to great achievements. Huntington even took his version of the frontier thesis one step farther than Turner; because of women's "more sensitive nervous organization," the frontier had influenced women *more* than men.[38]

Clearly, popular culture supplied questionable assumptions and suppositions to fill the void that Turner and other professional historians created. Purveyors of popular culture also failed to apply scholarly analysis and rigor to such larger questions as the significance of westward expansion to women; the effect of the frontier on women; whether the West provided a safety-valve for women, as Turner argued it had for men; or how Turner's frontier could have been democratic when it denied the female segment of its population the right to vote and hold office.[39] But so long as the field lay uncontested by scholars, popularizers enjoyed a relatively free hand.

Over time, of course, a number of historians began to recognize weaknesses in Turner's thesis and the limitations it imposed upon others. For instance, historian Charles Beard judged Turner's thesis as "too broad and sweeping" and noted the absence of organized labor in Turner's analysis.[40] Others called for consideration of Native Americans, Hispanics, African Americans, Germans and other immigrants, and such religious groups as Catholics, Mormons, and Presbyterians. Still others noted the absence of urban history, of regional geographical analysis, and of comparisons between the American West and other frontiers.[41] In 1964, historian David Potter indicted Turner for assuming that "the characteristics of American men are the characteristics of the American people, and that since women are people, the characteristics of the American people are the characteristics of American women."[42] Here at last Potter had revealed the lack of women and asked for their inclusion in studies of regionalism and the West.

In the meantime, a few scholars, such as Mary Hargreaves and T. A. Larson, began to study western women and pose questions concerning their lives.[43] During the mid-1970s, this growing interest in western women erupted in a series of conference papers, articles, and books. No longer content to allow popular culture to fabricate the lives of western women, a growing number of scholarly historians rejected Turner's male-oriented view of the West and began to write women into western history. Partly as a result of New Left criticism of historical scholarship in general, and partly due to the emergence of the contemporary feminist movement, historians of women began the long process of reconstructing the history of women in the West. Historians in both East and West soon devised a three-fold mission: to add women to the historical West, to revise popular culture images, and to develop sophisticated scholarship regarding western women.[44]

Unlike Turner, many of these scholars also attempted to analyze the significance of the frontier for women and assess the effects of westward expansion upon women. But they did not arrive at the conclusions Turner would have reached even if he had remembered women. Given Turner's outlooks, he would have surely categorized women along racial and ethnic lines, just as he did men. Thus, Native American women would have been "Indians," the receivers of "civilization," while Anglo women would have been "Americans," part of the advancing inculcators of "civilization." Because Turner concluded that the frontier built Americans' strength and independence, he presumably would have believed that the frontier also strengthened and liberated American women, at least Anglo-American women. Turner suggested as much in a 1926 study of pioneers' children. In one page devoted to daughters of the pioneers, Turner mentioned such successful women as Chicago reformer Jane Addams and Wisconsin suffragist Carrie Chapman Catt; he also noted that of the twelve women selected in 1925 as "the greatest women of America," one-third were daughters of pioneer families.[45]

Modern historians of women take a very different approach to western women, thus escaping what one historian has described as Turner's "mischievous" and "confining" influence.[46] While they consider dynamics, forces, and larger explanations, they also study groups and individuals. Consequently, they analyze the significance of the frontier and the effects of westward expansion on Native, Mexican, Anglo, African, and Asian American women; at the same time they recognize and respect individuality within those groups caused by social class, religion, age, education, marital status, and other factors.[47] Increasingly, historians of western women also maintain that they must study women before and after the advent of the frontier, that it formed only one part of western history.

Clearly, the revolution in women's status and recognition that Abigail Adams threatened in 1776 is well underway. Although John Adams ignored Abigail's counsel about including "the ladies" in the nation's new government and Frederick Jackson Turner evidently went unadvised on the matter of including them in western history, modern historians of western women agree with Abigail: the women must be remembered. These historians not only write women into the history of the West and revise popular images at every turn, but are also asking myriad questions about women in the West. Abigail's mutiny may have had to wait two hundred years, but scholars who decided that western women deserved their share of attention have launched a splendid insurrection. And if Turner the historian would have been puzzled, Turner the human being surely would have approved.

Notes

1. Carl Becker, "Kansas," in Guy Stanton Ford, ed., *Essays in American History Dedicated to Frederick Jackson Turner* (New York, 1951), 85–111; Frederic L. Paxson, "A Generation of the Frontier Hypothesis, 1893–1932," *Pacific Historical Review,* 2 (Mar. 1933), 34–51.

2. Herbert D. Croly, *The Promise of American Life* (New York, 1909), 3–7; Hamlin Garland, "The Passing of the Frontier," *The Dial,* 64 (Oct. 4, 1919), 285.

3. For a detailed account of Turner's life and work see Ray Allen Billington, *Frederick Jackson Turner: Historian, Scholar, Teacher* (New York, 1973).

4. Turner to Woodrow Wilson, Nov. 8, 1896, in Wilbur R. Jacobs, ed., *The Historical World of Frederick Jackson Turner, With Selections From His Correspondence* (New Haven, Conn., 1968), 27–28.

5. Quoted ibid., 12.

6. Turner to Max Farrand, June 23, 1905, ibid., 35, 37.

7. Louise Phelps Kellogg, "The Passing of a Great Teacher: Frederick Jackson Turner," *Historical Outlook,* 23 (Oct. 1932), 270–72; Kellogg, "Preface," in Frederick Jackson Turner, *The Early Writings of Frederick Jackson Turner,* ed. Fulmer Mood (Madison, Wisc., 1938), ix.

8. Turner to Constance Lindsay Skinner, Mar. 15, 1922, in Jacobs, ed., *Historical World of Turner,* 59.

9. Turner to Max Farrand, Sept. 27, 1908, ibid., 40–43.

10. Ray Allen Billington, ed., *"Dear Lady" The Letters of Frederick Jackson Turner and Alice Forbes Perkins Hooper, 1910–1932* (San Marino, Cal., 1970), 70, 27, 428. Billington also argued that Turner was a "good" and "sensitive" man in "Frederick Jackson Turner: The Image and the Man," *Western Historical Quarterly,* 3 (Apr. 1972), 137–52.

11. Wilbur R. Jacobs, ed., *Frederick Jackson Turner's Legacy: Unpublished Writings in American History* (1965; rep., Lincoln, Neb., 1977), 154.

12. Frederick Jackson Turner, "Dominant Forces in Western Life," *Atlantic Monthly,* 79 (Apr. 1987), 439.

13. Frederick Jackson Turner, "The Significance of the Frontier in American History," *American Historical Association Annual Report for the Year 1893* (Washington, D.C., 1894), 201.

14. See, for example, the listing of leaders in the American Historical Association in Clarence Winthrop Bowen, "Congress of American Scholars," *Harper's Weekly,* 8 (Dec. 25, 1909), 24–25.

15. Quoted in E. David Cronon, "Woodrow Wilson, Frederick Jackson Turner, and the State Historical Society of Wisconsin," *Wisconsin Magazine of History,* 71 (Summer 1988), 296. See also Woodrow Wilson, "The Making of a Nation," *Atlantic Monthly,* 80 (July 1897), 1–14; Wendell H. Stephenson, ed., "The Influence of Woodrow Wilson on Frederick Jackson Turner," *Agricultural History,* 19 (Oct. 1945), 249–53; and George C. Osborn, "Woodrow Wilson and Frederick Jackson Turner," *New Jersey Historical Society Proceedings,* 74 (July 1956), 208–29.

16. Ulrich Bonnell Phillips, "The Traits and Contributions of Frederick Jackson Turner," *Agricultural History,* 19 (Jan. 1945), 21–23.

17. Carl Becker, review of Frederick Jackson Turner, *The Frontier in American History,* in *The Nation,* 3 (Nov. 10, 1920), 536.

18. Lewis Mumford, "The Romanticism of the Pioneer," in *The Golden Day: A Study in American Experience and Culture* (New York, 1926), 47–81; Herman Clarence Nixon, "Precursors of Turner in the Interpretation of the American Frontier," *South Atlantic Quarterly,* 28 (Jan. 1929), 83–89; Lee Benson, "The Historical Background of Turner's Frontier Essay," *Agricultural History,* 25 (Apr. 1951), 59–82.

19. John Opie, "Frederick Jackson Turner, the Old West, and Formation of a National Mythology," *Environmental Review,* 5 (Summer 1981), 79–91; Vernon E. Mattson, "West as Myth," *Journal of the History of the Behavioral Sciences,* 24 (Jan. 1988), 9–12.

20. See Frederick Jackson Turner, "Social Forces in American History," *American Historical Review,* 16 (Jan. 1911), 217–33, for his definition of current issues and forces through which to study the past.

21. Turner to Merle Curti, Aug. 8, 1928, in Jacobs, ed., *Historical World of Turner,* 7.

22. Martin Ridge, "The American West: From Frontier to Region," *The New Mexico Historical Review,* 64 (Apr. 1989). See also Murray Kane, "Some Considerations on the Frontier Concept of Frederick Jackson Turner," *Mississippi Valley Historical Review,* 27 (Dec. 1940), 379–400, who maintains that Turner was an economic historian.

23. Fulmer Mood, "Turner's Formative Period," in Mood, ed., *Writings of Turner,* 20, 35.

24. Turner to Arthur M. Schlesinger, Apr. 18, 1922, in Jacobs, ed., *World of Turner,* 155.

25. William Cronon, "Turner's First Stand: The Significance of Significance in American History," in Richard W. Etulain, ed., *Writing Western History: Essays on Major Western Historians* (Albuquerque, 1991), 73–101.

26. Mood, "Turner's Formative Period," 12.

27. Joseph Schafer, "Turner's Early Writings," *Wisconsin Magazine of History,* 22 (Dec. 1938), 217.

28. Frederick Jackson Turner, "The Problem of the West," *Atlantic Monthly,* 78 (Sept. 1896), 289.

29. Frederick Jackson Turner, "The Colonization of the West, 1820–1830," *American Historical Review,* 11 (Jan. 1906), 303–27.

30. Jacobs, ed., *Turner's Legacy,* 170.

31. Frederick Jackson Turner, "Social Forces in American History," *American Historical Review,* 16 (Jan. 1911), 217–33.

32. Carl Becker, *Everyman His Own Historian: Essays on History and Politics* (New York, 1935), 214.

33. Jacobs, ed., *Turner's Legacy,* 153–55.

34. Lee Benson, "The Historian as Mythmaker: Turner and the Closed Frontier," in David M. Ellis, ed., *The Frontier in American Development: Essays in Honor of Paul Wallace Gates* (Ithaca, 1969), 3–19; Opie, "Frederick Jackson Turner," 79–91. For Turner's rhetorical powers, see Ronald H. Carpenter, "Wisconsin's Rhetorical Historians, Frederick Jackson Turner: A Review Essay," *Wisconsin Magazine of History,* 68 (Spring 1985), 199–203.

35. Jacobs, ed., *Turner's Legacy,* 81.

36. Turner to Constance Lindsay Skinner, Mar. 15, 1922, in Jacobs, ed., *Historical World of Turner,* 57.

37. Emeline Fuller, *Left by the Indians: Story of My Life* (Mount Vernon, Iowa, 1892).

38. Ellsworth Huntington, "Why the American Woman is Unique," *The Nation,* 125 (Aug. 3, 1927), 105–07.

39. Turner, "The Significance of the Frontier," 221.

40. Charles Beard's reviews of Turner's *The Frontier in American History,* in *The New Republic,* 79 (Feb. 16, 1921), 349–50, and "The Frontier in American History," ibid., 97 (Feb. 1939), 359–62.

41. For an overview of the fate of Turner's thesis after his death, see Howard R. Lamar, "Frederick Jackson Turner," in Marcus Cunliffe and Robin W. Winks, eds., *Pastmasters: Some Essays on American Historians* (New York, 1969), 74–109.

42. David M. Potter, "American Women and the American Character," in John A. Hague, ed., *American Character and Culture: Some Twentieth Century Perspectives* (Deland, Fla., 1964), 66. See also David M. Potter, *People of Plenty: Economic Abundance and the American Character* (Chicago, 1954), 206. Another leading historian who changed his mind about the Turner thesis was John D. Hicks, "Our Pioneer Heritage: A Reconsideration," *Prairie Schooner,* 30 (Winter 1956), 359–61.

43. Mary W. M. Hargreaves, "Homesteading and Homemaking on the Plains: A Review," *Agricultural History,* 47 (Apr. 1973), 156–63; Hargreaves, "Women in the Agricultural Settlement of the Northern Plains," *Agricultural History,* 50 (Jan. 1976), 5–16; T. A. Larson, "Dolls, Vassals, and Drudges — Pioneer Women in the West," *Western Historical Quarterly,* 3 (Jan. 1972), 5–16; Larson, "Women's Role in the American West," *Montana: The Magazine of Western History,* 24 (July 1974), 2–11.

44. Julie Roy Jeffrey, *Frontier Women: The Trans-Mississippi West, 1840–1880* (New York, 1979); John Mack Faragher, *Women and Men on the Overland Trail* (New Haven, 1979); Glenda Riley, "Images of the Frontierswomen: Iowa as a Case Study," *Western Historical Quarterly,* 8 (Apr. 1977), 189–202; Riley, *Frontierswomen: The Iowa Experience* (Ames, 1981); Sandra L. Myres, *Westering Women and the Frontier Experience, 1800–1915* (Albuquerque, 1982); Lillian Schlissel, *Women's Diaries of the Westward Journey* (New York, 1982); Elizabeth Jameson, "Women as Workers, Women as Civilizers: True Womanhood in the American West," *Frontiers,* 7 (1984), 1–8; Susan Armitage, "Women and Men in Western History: A Stereotypical Vision," *Western Historical Quarterly,* 16 (Oct. 1985), 380–95; Paula Petrik, "The Gentle Tamers in Transition: Women in the Trans-Mississippi West," *Feminist Studies,* 11 (Fall 1985), 677–94.

45. Frederick Jackson Turner, "The Children of the Pioneers," *Yale Review,* 15 (July 1926), 645–70.

46. Michael P. Malone, "Beyond the Last Frontier: Toward a New Approach in Western American History," *Western Historical Quarterly,* 20 (Nov. 1989), 409–27.

47. See, for example, Lawrence B. de Graaf, "Race, Sex, and Region: Black Women in the American West, 1850–1920," *Pacific Historical Review,* 49 (May 1980), 285–313; Yuji Ichioka, "*Amerika Nadeshiko:* Japanese Immigrant Women in the United States, 1900–1924," ibid., 339–57; Mario T. García, "The Chicana in American History: The Mexican Women of El Paso, 1880–1910 — A Case Study," ibid., 315–37; Jane Lecompte, "The Independent Women of Hispanic New Mexico, 1821–1846," *Western Historical Quarterly,* 12 (Jan. 1981), 17–35; Albert L. Hurtado, "Hardly a Farm House — A Kitchen Without Them: Indian and White Households on the California Borderland Frontier in 1860," *Western Historical Quarterly,* 13 (July 1982), 145–70; Vicki L. Ruiz, *Cannery Women, Cannery Lives: Mexican Women, Unionization, and the California Food Processing Industry, 1930–1950* (Albuquerque, 1987); Sarah Deutsch, *No Separate Refuge: Culture, Class, and Gender on an Anglo-Hispanic Frontier in the American Southwest, 1880–1940* (New York, 1987); Elizabeth Jameson, "Toward a Multicultural History of Women in the Western United States," *Signs,* 13 (Summer 1988), 761–91; Glenda Riley, "American Daughters: Black Women in the West," *Montana: The Magazine of Western History,* 38 (Spring 1988), 14–27; Frances R. Conly, "Marina Didn't Have a Covered Wagon: A Speculative Reconstruction," *The Californian,* 7 (Mar.–Aug. 1989), 4–54; and Antonia I. Castañeda, "Gender, Race, and Culture: Spanish-Mexican Women in the Historiography of Frontier California," *Frontiers,* 11 (1990), 8–20.

Martin Ridge

The Life of an Idea: The Significance of Frederick Jackson Turner's Frontier Thesis

In this straightforward, clearly written essay, Martin Ridge presents a brief overview of the content and influence of Turner's frontier essay. A student of the well-known frontier historian Ray Allen Billington, former editor of the *Journal of American History,* and long-time senior research associate at the Huntington Library, Ridge finds much to praise in Turner the man, writer, and thinker.

Part of Ridge's discussion treats Turner's role as an evangelist for American exceptionalism. As Ridge writes of Turner's ideas: "The frontier theory offered a reason for national uniqueness. It provided an explanation for American exceptionalism; the frontier was what made America and Americans — despite the multiple origins of immigrants — different from Europe and Europeans." Americans of Turner's time and many others since, Ridge contends, believed and continue to believe that the frontier experience is a key to understanding American identity.

Questions for a Closer Reading

1. The tone and content of Ridge's smoothly presented essay contrast with those in the essays by Richard White and Glenda Riley. In what specific ways does Ridge's point of view differ from theirs?

2. Do you think Ridge should be called a Turnerian (one who advocates or follows Turner's ideas)?

3. Would you consider the frontier essay a "masterpiece" in the sense that Ridge uses that word here?

4. Are you persuaded by Ridge's contentions about Turner and exceptionalism? Why or why not?

5. According to Ridge, what was the primary reason that Turner's frontier thesis caught on with historians and the general public?

The Life of an Idea: The Significance of Frederick Jackson Turner's Frontier Thesis

One of the favorite discussion topics among American historians is the question: what piece of American historical writing has been most influential in American life? Although the subject seems almost trivial, given serious thought it is a challenge. There are, after all, only a handful of historians whose work has reached beyond the "Halls of Ivy" and even fewer who seem to have had an impact on American culture. Such a group would include Charles A. Beard, Alfred Chandler, Oscar Handlin, Richard Hofstadter, Perry Miller, Samuel Eliot Morison, Francis Parkman, Arthur Schlesinger, Frederick Jackson Turner, and C. Vann Woodward, to name only the more prominent.

From the works of these authors, Frederick Jackson Turner's brief essay, "The Significance of the Frontier in American History," is the most logical choice for the most influential piece of historical writing. Turner's essay occupies a unique place in American history as well as in American historiography.[1] There is a valid reason for this. It, more than any other piece of historical scholarship, most affected the American's self and institutional

Martin Ridge, "The Life of an Idea: The Significance of Frederick Jackson Turner's Frontier Thesis," *Montana: The Magazine of Western History* 40 (Winter 1991): 2–13.

perceptions. "The Significance of the Frontier in American History" is, in fact, a masterpiece.

A masterpiece is not merely an outstanding work or something that identifies its creator as a master craftsman in the field. A masterpiece should change the way a public sees, feels, or thinks about reality. It should explicitly or implicitly tell much about its own times, but it should also cast a long shadow. It should have a significant impact on the way people at the time and afterward both perceive their world and act in it.

To look outside of history for an example and find an analogy in art, it may mean creating a new sense of reality — as Braque did with the development of cubism. All of the parts of a reality exist in a cubist work by Braque, but they compel the viewer to confront reality in a new way. The world of art has never been the same because of Braque. Some in the aesthetic community embraced it; others denounced it; Hitler and Stalin saw it as degenerate and banned it. A historical masterpiece should also strike fire. It must attract imitators but defy emulation. Ironically, a masterpiece must have not only these favorable attributes but also it must, as in the case of cubism, generate serious criticism and hostility. "The Significance of the Frontier in American History" did all these things.

From the time Turner's essay was published in the 1890s until today it has been the one piece of American historical writing that historians have praised, denounced, and tried to ignore. It has been called both a North Star and an albatross in American history. But even more importantly, its themes regarding American society and character as depicted in fiction, art, drama, and film have so effectively captured the American public's imagination and are now so deeply woven into the American consciousness that it may still be a part of the American mentality a century from now. It is worth noting, too, that today, almost at the one-hundredth anniversary of the essay's publication, the March 18, 1990, issue of the *New York Times Magazine* as well as the May 21, 1990, issue of *U.S. News and World Report* carried articles attacking it as if Turner were alive and prepared to defend himself. No other historical interpretation of American society has left so lasting a legacy.[2]

"The Significance of the Frontier in American History" is a profoundly personal as well as historical statement.[3] Frederick Jackson Turner, very much a product of the Middle West and Victorian America, was born in Portage, Wisconsin, in November 1861. His parents belonged to the nation's white, native-born, urban, middle-class elite; his father was a Republican politician, a promoter-investor in pioneer enterprises like railroads, and a newspaper editor-publisher; his mother had taught school. From his boyhood Turner learned liberal ideas from political table talk, listened to discussions about the economic potential of underdeveloped Wisconsin, and came to appreciate the power of the written and spoken word. Little wonder that when Turner entered the University of Wisconsin he considered journalism a proper career for an up-and-coming young man.

Turner's cultural baggage also included a keen recognition of his boyhood environment. Portage was no longer a backward Wisconsin town by nineteenth-century standards but a bustling community of about five thousand inhabitants. Tales of the Indians, fur traders, trappers, and Irish lumberjacks, who had made up the early history of the place, were still told in the streets. Later, Turner himself recounted that he had seen Indians being shipped off to a reservation, loggers tying up their rafts, and the victim of a lynch mob left hanging as an example to would-be wrongdoers. To live in Portage during the immediate post–Civil War years, for Turner, was to feel a part of the great surge of national energy that was subduing, taming, developing, exploiting, and making America. That powerful force was also Americanizing Wisconsin's immigrants. These people, especially the Germans who lived near Portage, were entering fully into American society and sharing both political power and economic opportunity.

More than people and events influenced Turner. He embraced an implicit contradiction: on the one hand he took pride in American economic development, while on the other hand he felt that the American wilderness was a limitless pristine Garden of Eden, a view fashioned by his familiar Wisconsin countryside, with its sparkling brooks, its fish-filled lakes, its pristine piney forests. It is wrong to assume that Turner's response to the wilderness was naive Emersonianism. In a very real sense Turner never abandoned the countryside, even when he taught at Harvard or retired among the citrus groves at the Huntington Library in California. Turner never escaped his contradictory belief in an Edenic vision of underdeveloped America, which he both praised and tried to reconcile with his faith in economic progress.

The University of Wisconsin was a small land-grant college in 1880 when Turner arrived in Madison. As an unusually bright, highly motivated, articulate, well-bred youngster from a good small-town family, he was very successful. He joined a social fraternity, edited the school paper, engaged in debates, and walked off with the prestigious Burrows Prize, the most coveted oratorical award the university could bestow. This was at a time when the college orator rather than the college athlete was the campus hero. Although he read widely and studied rhetoric, his first love was history; and he was profoundly influenced by Professor William F. Allen, a Harvard-educated, German-trained scholar of ancient and medieval history who was the university's first and sole professor of history.

Graduated in 1884, the year the American Historical Association was organized, Turner briefly tried journalism, working for the Milwaukee *Journal* and the Chicago *Inter-Ocean,* before returning to Wisconsin to prepare for a teaching career. The decision to become a historian was a courageous one because jobs were scarce — Wisconsin had only one history professor — and a potential faculty member needed both Ph.D. and considerable skill as a lecturer. While a graduate student at Wisconsin, Turner taught rhetoric — which was then public speaking and composition — and history.

After earning a master's degree, he moved on to Johns Hopkins University for a doctorate because it was the best place to study. The Johns Hopkins faculty, German in training or scholarly orientation, played a major role in introducing the critical seminar to America. At Hopkins, Turner rubbed shoulders with fellow graduate students and studied with professors who were to be the scholarly giants of the age: Charles Homer Haskins, Woodrow Wilson, J. Franklin Jameson, Richard T. Ely, and Herbert Baxter Adams.

The faculty and students at Hopkins worked in an atmosphere of zealotry approaching a religious revival. Determined to make the writing and teaching of history into a true profession, convinced that they could find and propound objective truth, they sought to create a new discipline of history that was based on larger knowledge and a more rigorous method of research.[4] They were exposed to the works of leading European scholars. Turner thrived in this environment, where no assumption was sacred and where ideas were shared, debated, and openly criticized.

The Hopkins history department, however, was not free of doctrine. Herbert Baxter Adams, its dominant figure, espoused the so-called "germ theory," which explained historical development more in terms of origins than of dynamics.[5] Therefore, according to Adams, American institutions were merely an extension of medieval Teutonic structures that had been transferred first to England and then to North America. His thinking was compatible with that of the major literary scholars of the period, who were busy tracing historical linkages between Anglo-Saxon and English literature as it was taught in American schools. This approach was virtually sterile to historians deeply interested in their own past, however, because it denied the possibility that anything original or unique could stem from the American experience.

When Turner returned to Wisconsin in 1889, where the untimely death of his mentor, William F. Allen, opened the way for his advancement, he carried with him all the skills, zeal, and goals acquired at Hopkins. But he also brought with him both a profound faith in, and emerging doubts about, how to study American history. He slowly distanced himself from Herbert Baxter Adams' view of history and changed his perception of how to understand the past. He accepted the broadest conception of history — denying that it was merely past politics or the activities of only elite groups — and insisted that historians should not overlook the doings of the "degraded tillers of the soil."[6] Yet he was loath to abandon Adams' position completely because he still believed in historical continuity but was sorely troubled by how to unite the present and the past. Turner, like others of his generation, believed that objective historical scholarship could serve a higher purpose. Thus, Turner wrestled with severe intellectual problems in his early years of teaching and writing. Adams' interpretation not only led away from any analysis of a national entity but also conflicted with Turner's personal experience, with his interest in his native Middle West, and with his historical imagination.

Several generations of scholars have sought to determine exactly how and when Turner changed his ideas and how they evolved. They have searched for the sources of his thought in his reading notes and clipping files, his day book, his rhetorical studies, and his teaching. Some historians argued that the ideas he expressed were so common that they were in the air — everybody was thinking and talking about them.[7] But as far as Turner was concerned, one thing is clear — his genius lay in a mind that was capable of what psychologists identify as both convergent and divergent thinking. Convergent thinking is required in areas of compelling inferences — in seeking solutions to questions. Divergent thinking is important for breaking new ground. These qualities were demanded of him when Herbert Baxter Adams recommended that he present a paper at the World Congress of Historians to be held during the Chicago World's Columbian Exposition in July 1893.

Turner, at age thirty-one, probably under hurried conditions because he was a procrastinator, wrote " The Significance of the Frontier in American History."[8] It is far more a manifesto, albeit a very florid one, than a piece of research. He called on Americans to turn away from the accepted paradigms of their past. "Our early history," he conceded in a nod to his graduate school mentor, Herbert Baxter Adams, "is the study of European germs developing in an American environment." But he added, "Too exclusive attention has been paid by institutional students to the Germanic origins; too little to the American factors." He was equally critical of the constitutional historian Hermann Von Holst of the University of Chicago and the gifted amateur James Ford Rhodes for overemphasizing slavery and politics. In this way he eliminated two rival paradigms for understanding American development.

Turner said more: he called on historians to recognize the major American historical discontinuity of their own time. To dramatize this disfunction Turner quoted from the report of the Superintendent of the Census, who pointed out that by 1890 it was no longer possible, as it had been since 1790, to indicate on a map of the United States the existence of a frontier line of settlement. This simple statement, he asserted, marked "the closing of a great historic movement. Up to our own day," he wrote, "America has been in large degree the history of the colonization of the Great West." And he added, "The existence of an area of free land . . . and the advance of American settlement westward, explain American development." Turner left the definition of the frontier vague — "The term is an elastic one," he wrote, but the most significant thing about the frontier was that it existed "at the hither edge of free land." The frontier was one of several vital forces behind constitutional forms, "that call these organs into life," he wrote, "and shape them to meet changing conditions."

The nation's institutions owed their originality to the fact that they had been "compelled to adapt themselves to the changes of an expanding people — to the changes involved in crossing a continent, in winning a wilderness, and in developing at each area of this progress, out of the primitive economic and political conditions of the frontier, the complexity of city life." The reconstruction of society made the frontier — "the meeting point between savagery and civilization" — the area of the "most rapid and effective Americanization."

The frontier helped create a new people and new institutions. Americans were a mixed race, as the term was used at the close of the nineteenth century. Newcomers on the frontier, whether from abroad or from different parts of the country, were integrated into a new American economic and political community, a process that redefined their cultural and national identity. They were "English in neither nationality nor characteristics." Frontier conditions made everyone more national than parochial because only the central government had the power to care for its new communities, build roads, provide for law and order, maintain an army to control Indians, and above all subsidize the economies of new regions. "Loose construction of the Constitution," resulted and, Turner argued, "increased as the nation marched westward." The Louisiana Purchase was an outstanding example.

A principal function of the frontier, as Turner saw it, was the "promotion of democracy here and in Europe." He espoused the ideas that political democracy and land ownership were virtually inseparable. His frontier democracy was "born of free land," which resulted in the distribution of both political power and economic opportunity more equally than it had been in any country in the western world. This was part of a process that transformed the concept of Jeffersonian republicanism into the national republicanism of James Monroe and ultimately into the democracy of Andrew Jackson.

For Turner, America's political democracy reflected its frontier origins. It displayed the independent spirit of a landed class rather than the subservience of a peasant class. American democracy was strong in selfishness and individualism, intolerant of administrative experience and education, and tended to press individual liberty beyond its proper bounds. It encouraged lawlessness, lax business honor, harmful currency policies. These behaviors, Turner pointed out, alarmed the less democratic East and resulted in severe tensions and conflict between the East and the West. In a sense, Turner implicitly argued that sectional conflict rather than class conflict was more significant in American history. He believed that the struggle on the frontier to redistribute political power and economic resources was one of the major issues in the nineteenth century.

Turner also sought out national traits spawned on the frontier that distinguished Americans from Europeans. In this context he wrote, "To the frontier the American intellect owes its striking characteristics": "coarseness and strength combined with acuteness and inquisitiveness"; a "practical, inventive turn of mind, quick to find expedients"; a concentration on material things but a lack of concern for the aesthetic; a "restless, nervous energy"; a "dominant individualism, working for good and for evil"; and, foremost among all these, the optimism and enthusiasm that came with the freedom of choice and place. These traits, he observed, were bred into the American people by three centuries of frontier experience.

In conclusion Turner returned to his original theme of historical discontinuity: the frontier era was at an end. He posed the critical question: what would happen to the United States without a frontier? As Turner's most impassioned advocate of the past generation, Ray Allen Billington, put it: "Never again would nature yield its gifts so generously. Never again would a stubborn environment help break the bonds of custom and summon mankind to accept its conditions. No longer would frontiering," as Turner saw it, "'furnish a new field of opportunity, a gate to escape from the bondage of the past.'" Now Americans would have to manage their economy and their politics in order to live in a closed-space world.[9] For Turner, the first period of American history had ended with the closing of the frontier.

In asking Americans to reconsider their history through the prism of the frontier Turner did several things. First, he produced a radical manifesto for historians. Second, he advocated a theory of secular, democratic, American exceptionalism. Third, he asserted that the American people were a unique nationality or race, as the term was used at that time, with distinctive cultural traits based primarily on their own experience and not Teutonic antecedents. The unstated leitmotif of his essay was a strident chauvinism. Fourth, he claimed that the essence of American identity was not to be found in the New England Puritan mind or in the mentality of the former slaveholding tidewater South but among people on the moving frontier. Fifth, he insisted on the existence of a historical disjunction — the nation stood on the threshold of a new age: the story of how the frontier formed America remained to be written. And finally, he recognized that America in the 1890s represented the end product of a triumphal if bloody march of a pioneering people from a cluster of New England villages and tidewater plantations across the continent. Moreover, in a Darwinian sense it depicted a national evolutionary process from a simple extractive and pastoral entity to a complex urban organism. The essay was written in the idiom of modern evolutionary science.

More is the pity the voices of race, class, and gender were muted or absent in Turner's essay. This did not mean that Turner had sanitized the westering experience. It means that he legitimated the use of the frontier to explain the nation's history for wider audiences from the perspective of his generation and his personal experience.

If Turner expected anger or anguish from historians who held a dissenting view, he was surely disappointed for the immediate response to the essay was initial silence followed by an academic yawn. There was no discussion. There was not even a ripple. Turner repeated the paper at a December 1893 meeting of the State Historical Society of Wisconsin, after which it was published by the Society. Turner also published it in The American Historical Association's *Annual Report* for 1893.

When Turner mailed copies to distinguished historians, newspaper and magazine editors, and other people of note, as some young professors and self-publicists are wont to do, the results were almost predictable. Theodore Roosevelt praised Turner for stating clearly the "thought that has been floating around rather loosely." Francis A. Walker, president of the Massachusetts Institute of Technology and a leading statistician, praised the title — he may have read no further. Achille Loria, the Italian economist whose work Turner had read and referred to, applauded Turner for substantiating his views. John Fiske, perhaps the most successful popular historian of the period, told Turner the essay was excellent — he too was working along the same line. Turner's biographer notes that the typical remark of eastern historians was that "Turner must be a very provincial type of historian."[10]

Turner's essay was anything but provincial in intent and scope. He offered a sophisticated holistic interpretation of American history and provided a unifying hypothesis around which to organize the study of the United States in the nineteenth century. But one need not be a Freudian psychoanalyst to realize that Turner's essay represented the most obvious personal experiences in Portage and the University of Wisconsin, his faith in national growth and progress, his identification with the geography of his region, his insistence on the contributions of the near recent past, as well as his scholarship and his historical imagination.

No doubt, this same feeling stirred other members of his generation who were born or reared beyond the Appalachians, and it accelerated the widespread acceptance of his theory. State and local historians, whether in colleges, universities, museums, or historical societies, for the first time understood how their work fit into the broader context of American history and could take pride in their contributions to history. Why study Teutonic germs that said little of the present when there was so much to be told about the contributions of local or regional men and women whose exploits could be recalled by living people? The earliest period of exploration, settlement, and development — the nineteenth-century frontier era — loomed large in its own right as a field of study. Courses in the "History of the West" or the "History of the Frontier" cropped up in colleges and universities not only where Turner's students taught but also throughout the nation as historians became familiar with his ideas. The ideas expressed in the "Significance of the Frontier in American History" may have been "floating around loosely" as Theodore Roosevelt put it, but their acceptance came first among people who felt themselves like the westering men and women who wanted to escape eastern hegemony. The implications of Turner's thesis were not lost on geographers, economists, and political scientists who picked up on the idea of the frontier and used it in their work.

Within a decade and a half of Turner's presentation at Chicago, he had captured most of the citadels of the profession. He was sought after to lecture on any aspect of the frontier, to sign contracts to write text books and monographs, and to accept permanent appointment at Berkeley, Chicago, Stanford, and Harvard. His seminar at Wisconsin attracted gifted students, and he made the history department a powerhouse within the school. In 1910, for a variety of reasons including a head-to-head clash with the trustees of the university over the issue of intercollegiate football, he accepted a post at Harvard.

Ideas filtered through the medium of college courses are not rapidly disseminated, even in our own age. Turner's frontier hypothesis, however, far more quickly than many other revisionist theories, escaped the academy and entered the marketplace of ideas. There are many reasons for this. Turner popularized his ideas by writing for the *Atlantic Monthly* and reviewing books for other magazines.[11] He gave countless public lectures and became a featured speaker at commencement exercises. But the primary reason that the frontier idea took hold was that it made sense to the average citizen because it elevated the achievement of ordinary settlers.

Yet there was a more profound reason why the frontier idea appealed to the American people. It provided a usable history for a people who were increasingly aware of their emerging role in world leadership and equally self-conscious of the brevity of their national identity. The frontier experience also provided an American past as grand as that of England or any continental power, an American landscape as spectacular as any in the world, and heroes, heroines, and myths equal to any in Europe. In point of fact, they were often the same myths transposed. The frontier theory offered a reason for national uniqueness. It provided an explanation for American exceptionalism; the frontier was what made America and Americans — despite the multiple origins of immigrants — different from Europe and Europeans.

Turner's perception of the assimilation of various ethnic groups was part of this, not only because the frontier was an ethnic melting pot but also because it provided individuals who had moved West alone or in family groups with a link to a specific experience — such as traveling Zane's Trace, the National Road, the Overland Trail, the trek to Zion, or the Gold Rush — that was shared by others who could relate to the same westering experience. The Americans of Turner's day and in subsequent generations, like the frontier traders, soldiers, and settlers he visualized as conquering a continent, "had a blind eye for hard truths and a clear one for great expectations."[12]

The pervasiveness, dilution, and mythologizing of Turner's ideas about the frontier during the past century is almost impossible to describe. The novelist has remained the primary popularizer of an exaggerated if not distorted view of Turner's American exceptionalism by utilizing the frontier as the setting for an increasingly subtle morality play emphasizing the significance of the frontier's contradictory characterization of individualism, senseless yet essential nature of violence, and the ambiguous role of the exploitation of natural resources as basic themes. The number of novels based in a western setting that emphasized Turnerian themes is beyond calculation. They range from Emerson Hough's genteel Victorian pieces, A. B. Guthrie, and Wallace Stegner, to Louis L'Amour, E. L. Doctorow, and Larry McMurtry, who all depict a real West. Ironically, the stripping away of the romance of the frontier in contemporary novels — and Turner's rhetorical style contributed to establishing it — merely reinforces the perennial interest in the westering experience.

Turner would no doubt be aghast at how Hollywood, whether John Ford or Mel Brooks, and especially television have both popularized and trivialized his ideas about regional conflict, frontier types, lawlessness, and free land. Both have taken what should be considered vocational archetypes — such as the cowboy — and turned them into stereotypes in the worst sense. But even the cynical criticism that exists in contemporary film that makes anti-heroes of protagonists has not shattered the Turnerian model; it has simply reinforced the idea that the frontier was the vital factor that makes diversity an essential part of the American character.

Evidence of the pervasiveness of Turnerian rhetoric is so widespread that it has entered all aspects of American life. President Franklin D. Roosevelt used the closing of the frontier in a speech justifying a call for more economic planning. Both the domestic and foreign press depicted former

President Ronald Reagan and President George Bush as either western bad-men or steely-eyed sheriffs because of their foreign policy decisions. President John F. Kennedy saw space as a frontier. Americans call all areas of exploration and opportunity frontiers and speak of frontiers in medicine, physics, or even dentistry. No other nation in the world uses the word frontier as Americans do. Other peoples say frontier when they mean a border between nations.

There was no counterrevolution to Turnerianism in American historical writing — no one defended the "germ theory" per se, although a later generation of legal historians have reconstructed a version of it by emphasizing the taught tradition of law.[13] Over the years, however, the number and variety of attacks on the frontier thesis have been legion. Some historians seem to have made it a career choice. Oddly enough, the very vitriolic nature of the criticism, and its attending publicity have promoted continuing public awareness of the frontier influence on American life.

Turner's masterpiece, like Braque's cubist work — "Man with a Guitar" — has achieved a special place in American culture. It changed a vital part of the scholarly community, and its rhetoric has been absorbed into our every-day language. It changed the way most Americans continue to see themselves and their institutions. Moreover, it changed the way they are seen by others throughout the world. People who have never read "The Significance of the Frontier in American History" or heard of Frederick Jackson Turner — as is true of Braque and cubism — identify with it and recognize in it portions of a reality.

No other piece of American historical writing so legitimated the American historical imagination, stimulated so thorough an inquiry, precipitated so furious a dispute over so long a period, and embedded itself so deeply into the American psyche. To think of the history of "The Significance of the Frontier in American History" is to be reminded of a familiar passage from Christopher Marlowe's play, *Dr. Faustus:*

> "Was this the face that launch'd a thousand ships,
> And burnt the topless towers of Ilium?"

In the case of Turner's masterpiece, the answer is yes.

Notes

1. For a discussion of this subject, see Richard Hofstadter and Seymour Martin Lipset, *Turner and the Sociology of the Frontier* (New York: Basic Books, 1968); Richard Hofstadter, *The Progressive Historians: Turner, Beard, Parrington* (New York: Alfred A. Knopf, 1968); and David Noble, *The End of American History* (Minneapolis: University of Minnesota Press, 1985).

2. Frederick Jackson Turner was not a prolific author. He wrote two books: *Rise of the New West, 1819–1829* (New York: Harper and Brothers, 1906) and *The United States, 1830–1850: The Nation and its Sections* (New York: Henry Holt and Company, 1935). His major essays are gathered in two volumes: *The Frontier in American History* (New York: Henry Holt and Company, 1920) and *The Significance of Sections in American History* (New York: Henry Holt and Company, 1932). For an annotated list of Turner's works and publications dealing with the frontier, see Vernon E. Mattson and William E. Marion, *Frederick Jackson Turner: A Reference Guide* (Boston: G. K. Hall, 1985).

3. For bibliographical information regarding Turner, see Ray Allen Billington, *Frederick Jackson Turner: Historian, Scholar, Teacher* (New York: Oxford University Press, 1973).

4. For a discussion of the rise of the scientific objectivist school of historians, see Peter Novick, *That Noble Dream: The "Objectivity Question" and the American Historical Profession* (Cambridge, Mass.: Cambridge University Press, 1988).

5. Herbert Baxter Adams was not only a power within the profession but also a "master promoter" who helped organize the American Historical Association. See David D. Van Tassel, *Recording America's Past: An Interpretation of the Development of Historical Studies in America, 1607–1884* (Chicago: University of Chicago Press, 1960), 171.

6. Martin Ridge, ed., "The Significance of History" in, *Frederick Jackson Turner: Wisconsin's Historian of the Frontier* (Madison: State Historical Society of Wisconsin, 1986), 51. Turner's continuing interest in studying the lives of ordinary people is captured in a 1923 letter to Dr. Theodore Blegen where he used within quotation marks the phrase "history from the bottom up." There is some irony in the fact that the phrase was popular in the 1960s among radical social historians who rejected Turnerian thinking. Jesse Lemisch was probably unaware of its origin. See FJT to Blegen, March 16, 1923, Turner Papers, Huntington Library, San Marino, California.

7. For example, see Lee Benson, "The Historical Background of Turner's Frontier Essay," *Agricultural History,* 25 (April 1951), 59–82; Lee Benson, "Achille Loria's Influence on American Economic Thought, Including his Contribution to the Frontier Hypothesis," *Agricultural History,* 24 (October 1950), 182–99; Ray Allen Billington, *The Genesis of the Frontier Thesis: A Study of Historical Creativity* (San Marino: Huntington Library, 1971); and Ronald H. Carpenter, *The Eloquence of Frederick Jackson Turner* (San Marino: Huntington Library, 1983).

8. All of the quotations used are taken from Ridge, ed., "The Significance of the Frontier in American History," in *Frederick Jackson Turner: Wisconsin's Historian of the Frontier.* The history of the publication, republication, and exhibition of the essay is reported in James P. Danky, "A Bibliographical Note," ibid., 63–65.

9. Billington, *Frederick Jackson Turner,* 128.

10. Ibid., 129–30.

11. For Turner's role as a reviewer, see Martin Ridge, "A More Jealous Mistress: Frederick Jackson Turner as a Book Reviewer," *Pacific Historical Review,* 55 (February 1986), 49–63.

12. Ridge, *Frederick Jackson Turner: Wisconsin's Historian of the Frontier,* 8.

13. For an example of this in the field of frontier history, see John Phillip Reid, *Law for the Elephant: Property and Social Behavior on the Overland Trail* (San Marino: Huntington Library, 1980).

5. Will region replace frontier?

Donald Worster

New West, True West: Interpreting the Region's History

If Turner's thesis or the concept of a westward-moving frontier is no longer acceptable, as many historians have argued since the 1960s, how should the West be interpreted? As a developing region, contends Donald Worster, Hall Distinguished Professor of History at the University of Kansas. Rather than follow the *process* idea central to the frontier thesis, Worster argues, historians should return to the earlier interpretations of the historian Walter Prescott Webb, who depicted the American West as a separate, evolving *place*.

A leading environmental historian, Worster calls for more scholarly attention to "ecological modes." In his view, students should examine "how a people or peoples acquired a place and, then, how they perceived and tried to make use of it." Next, one must "identify the survival techniques they [newcomers] adopted, their patterns of work and economy, and their social relationships." Moving well beyond the earlier people-land relationships Turner mentioned, Worster calls for a study of the West that encompasses the region's "total history." In particular he calls attention to "pastoral" (grazing) and "hydraulic" (irrigation and reclamation) modes as essential for understanding the modern American West.

Questions for a Closer Reading

1. On occasion, Worster, like Patricia Nelson Limerick in the following selection, uses personal experience to buttress his arguments. How do you react to his statement

that he "know[s] in [his] bones that the regional rather than the frontier approach is 'right'"?

2. Are there topics other than the pastoral and hydraulic modes that must be addressed to understand the West as an identifiably unique region?

3. Might the concepts "frontier" and "region" pollinate one another to produce yet another way of interpreting the frontier and the American West? If so, what might that new interpretive point of view be?

New West, True West: Interpreting the Region's History

I say to my colleague in Chinese studies that I teach western history. "Doesn't almost everyone in this department," he complains. "The history of England, Germany, France, Italy — it is all western history in our courses. Nobody here knows or cares anything about the East." I cut him short to explain that what I mean by the West is not Europe, not the whole of western civilization. My West is the *American* West: that fabled land where the restless pioneer moves ever forward, settling one frontier after another; where the American character becomes self-reliant, democratic, and endlessly eager for the new; where we strip off the garments of civilization and don a rude buckskin shirt; where millions of dejected immigrants gather from around the world to be rejuvenated as Americans, sounding together a manly, wild, barbaric yawp of freedom. That is my West: precisely that and nothing more. "Oh," my colleague ventures, more perplexed now than cantankerous, "you mean 'the West' — the frontier, Indians, Clint Eastwood?" I nod vaguely and sidle off. It is all so hard to convey over a single, polite glass of academic sherry.

For a field that has been around so long, western American history can be

Donald Worster, "New West, True West: Interpreting the Region's History," *Western Historical Quarterly* 18 (April 1987): 141–56.

frustratingly difficult to pin down. Soon it will be a full century old. Often, with such advanced age comes a clarity of purpose as well as a record of achievement. Not so in this case. The record is impressive enough: the field now has several excellent journals, regularly holds good scholarly conferences, and boasts an immense bibliography that no one could read in a lifetime. But as for clarity of purpose, the field is still groping about in adolescence. It doesn't quite know who it is or what it wants to be when it grows up. What are its boundaries? Where is "West" and where is not? There is still no settled, mature answer.

There is, to be sure, an established body of writing about the history of the West, and usually it would be to such a body that we would turn for resolving what the field of study is or ought to be. In this case, however, the traditional literature is more a cause of confusion than a remedy. For it reveals that the West is just about anything that anyone has ever wanted it to be. That it has been located anywhere and everywhere.

My own private confusions of place may, in their ordinariness, illustrate that wonderful ambiguity we sense about the field. I was born in the Mohave Desert of southern California, an area the books say is indubitably part of the West. I grew up on the Great Plains, and again the books tell me that that is West too. But when I moved some years ago to Hawaii, was I still in the West or was I out of it? For an answer I might consult the *Western Historical Quarterly,* which reassures me in its index to recent articles in the field that the islands do indeed belong. The Hawaiian monarchs, resplendent in their feather capes and fed on taro, mullet, and the milk of coconuts, are to be understood (whatever their personal views of the matter) as having lived in the American West alongside Chief Sitting Bull and Geronimo; while Captain James Cook of Yorkshire was as much a western adventurer as Meriwether Lewis or John Charles Fremont. Now then, go to the other geographical extreme of the country. Move, as I have recently done, five thousand miles from Honolulu to the small Massachusetts town of Concord, founded in 1653 as the first inland settlement of the Bay colony. You will learn that it too, is, or has been, in the realm of the West! The authorities have it so. For example, that grand and indispensable reference work, *The Reader's Encyclopedia of the American West,* includes an entry on the settlement of Massachusetts, and it is a longer entry than the one on the Oregon Trail.[1] Thus, you may go west or east, young man or woman, and you will always in fact be going west.

As defined by its historians, the West has been nothing less than all of America, or all that we have conquered. For further evidence of how the part has swallowed the whole, consider the last work of the Harvard historian Frederick Merk, *A History of the Westward Movement,* published in 1978, one year after his death. He might as well have called it the story of the nation. There are chapters on Indian culture, cotton growing in the South, the Dred Scott decision, the industrialization of the Great Lakes, the Tennessee Valley Authority, and farm policy in the Kennedy-Johnson years. After more than six hundred pages of tracking American development, Professor Merk, in his moving peroration, expands even further his notion of the West as an "open frontier" to sweep in all of science and technology, all human control over the environment, all "the relations of man to his fellow man." "This is the frontier," he concludes, "now challenging the national energies."[2] If we follow his reasoning, the West is to be found wherever there is optimism, a love of freedom and democracy, an indomitable will to overcome all obstacles, a determination to make things better for the future. That is, I will grant you, the state of Oregon he is describing, but it also might be Australia or Hong Kong.

But hold: there is still more to the West than we have yet fathomed. Long before there was Merk's cotton gin, long before there was a colony planted on the cold Massachusetts shore in the seventeenth century, long before America was even discovered and named, the historians tell us of an even more ancient, shadowy West. On its existence we have, for example, the magisterial authority of the man who, until his death in 1981, was regarded by many as the dominant name in western history: Ray Allen Billington, senior research associate at the Huntington Library. His textbook, *Westward Expansion: A History of the American Frontier,* may be taken as one of the most authoritative delineations of the field. According to this book (4th ed., 1974), the American West was merely "the last stage in a mighty movement of peoples that began in the twelfth century when feudal Europe began pushing back the barbaric hordes" pressing in on Christendom. The Crusaders, off to do battle with the Moslems, were the first pioneers, and Jerusalem was their frontier. They did not prevail, but after them came the more triumphant Marco Polo, Christopher Columbus, and Ponce de Leon — came a whole multitude pushing the domain of the West out to the remote corners of the earth. In Billington's account the great saga rolls along for eight centuries, until it reaches the American Populists defending themselves against "ruthless exploitation of eastern interests." If I have the story right, there is an undeniable grandeur to it, stretching as it does from the armies of Richard the Lionhearted to those of old Sockless Jerry Simpson in droughty, dusty Kansas. My grandfather, himself a raggletaggle populist with tobacco juice streaming from his mouth, would have loved it. But then, just as we are ready to spring with Billington into the future, the grandeur abruptly fades away. With the defeat of the Populists in 1896, he declares in one of his last chapters, the West came to a sad death. It will have no more history to make in the twentieth century. Once the West was going every-where, now it is gone.[3]

To discover where the American West is supposed to be, I have been con-sulting major books published within the last ten or twelve years, books by scholars of stature from whom we have learned much. But having read them, I could not put my finger on the map and say, "There is the West." The books have attached too abstract a meaning to the word, so abstract in fact that it has become bewildering. The West is "movement," "expansion," the "frontier," they all say, and apparently any kind of movement, any ex-pansion, any frontier will do.

The primal source of this abstractness, this elusiveness of subject, must be located in the mind of the scholar who has gotten so much praise for im-agining the field in the first place: Frederick Jackson Turner. He started his-torians down a muddy, slippery road that ultimately leads to a swamp. That destination was not apparent for a long time. The route signs Turner put up had a deceptively concrete promise to them. In a letter written in the 1920s, he pointed out that "the 'West' with which I dealt, was a *process* rather than a fixed geographical region."[4] Earlier, he had made the same distinction in the notes for his Harvard course on the West: it was described as "a study of selected topics in the history of the West considered as a process rather than an area." The process, he explained in an unpublished essay, included:

1. the spread of settlement steadily westward, and

2. all the economic, social, and political changes involved in the exis-tence of a belt of free land at the edge of settlement;

3. the continual settling of successive belts of land;

4. the evolution of these successive areas of settlement through various stages of backwoods life, ranching, pioneer farming, scientific farm-ing, and manufacturing life.[5]

In short, Turner's "process" was really four of them, or rather, was a tangled web of many processes, all going on at once and including the whole development of American agriculture and industry, the history of popula-tion growth and movement, the creation of national institutions, and, some-where in the tangle, the making of an American personality type. No won-der western history has ever after had trouble staying on track.

When you are lost, the most sensible strategy is to go back to the point of departure, back where Mr. Turner once stood pointing the way, and look for another road. Ignore the signs saying, "[t]his way to process," and look in-stead for the one reading, "[T]o a fixed geographical region." Or better yet, look for the specific processes that went on in the specific region. We may grope and argue a lot along that way too, but we won't end up back in Massachusetts befuddled by Puritan theology or back with the Crusaders defeated and dead.

My strategy of diverging from Turner and his frontier theme is hardly original. It was implicitly recommended almost thirty years ago, in a 1957 article published in *Harper's Magazine,* by a man then described as "the West's leading historian," Walter Prescott Webb. The article was entitled "The American West: Perpetual Mirage." Had it been taken more fully to heart, it might have started the field off in a more promising direction. There was absolutely nothing in it of Turner's vaporous notion of the West as frontier advance. On the contrary, Webb gave the West a set of firm coordinates on the North American landscape. In his second paragraph he declared,

> Fortunately, the West is no longer a shifting frontier, but a region that can be marked off on a map, traveled to, and seen. Everybody knows when he gets there. It starts in the second tier of states west of the Big River.[6]

The West, in other words, begins with the Dakotas, Nebraska, Kansas, Oklahoma, and Texas. So defined, the West would become, along with the North and the South, one of the three great geographical regions of the coterminous United States.

In Webb's view, what sets this western region off from the other two major regions is the lack of enough rainfall to sustain traditional, European-derived agriculture. In that second tier of states the average yearly precipitation falls below the twenty-inch minimum needed to grow crops in the accustomed way. From there to the California coast the region is mainly dry: in its extremes it is a desert, elsewhere it is a subhumid environment. Admittedly, within it are some anomalies and further diversities — the Pacific northwest coast outstanding among them — which, for the sake of analysis, Webb had to ignore. Every region is, after all, only a generalization and is subject to exceptions.

This more mappable West, as everyone in the field knows, was an idea Webb took from the nineteenth-century explorer John Wesley Powell, whose *Report on the Lands of the Arid Region of the United States,* published in 1878 as a House of Representatives document, identified the 100th meridian as the line roughly dividing a humid from a subhumid America.[7] Webb nudged the line eastward a couple of degrees so it lay right outside Austin, Texas, where he lived. And he boldly declared that Powell's arid region was one and the same as the American West. For the post–World War Two generation, he sensed, the two regions had merged completely, and historians had better acknowledge the fact and stop harking back to Turner.

I know in my bones, if not always through my education, that Webb was right. His notion of the West as the arid region of the country fits completely my own experience and understanding. Born eighty years to the day after Frederick Jackson Turner — on the 14th of November, 1941 (Turner was born on the 14th of November, 1861) — I have never been able to think of the West as Turner did, as some process in motion. Instead, I think of it as a distinct place inhabited by distinct people: people like my parents, driven out of western Kentucky by dust storms to an even hotter, drier life in Needles, California, working along the way in flyblown cafes, fruit orchards, and on railroad gangs, always feeling dwarfed by the bigness of the land and by the economic power accumulated there. In my West, there are no coonskin caps, nor many river boats, axes, or log cabins. Those things all belong to another time, and another place — to an eastern land where nature offered an abundance of survival resources near at hand. My West is, by contrast, the story of men and women trying to wrest a living from a condition of severe natural scarcity and, paradoxically, of trying to survive in the midst of entrenched wealth.

This picture of the West, I submit, is closer to the one most western historians carry around in their heads today. When pushed hard to make a stand, we usually line up with Webb and Powell, not Turner. For instance, on the first page or so of the introduction to his book *Historians and the American West,* Michael Malone grants that he means by the West more or less what Webb meant: "the entire region lying west of the 98th meridian, the line of diminishing rainfall which runs from the eastern Dakotas on the north through central Texas on the south."[8] But having admitted that much to ourselves, we often resist the logical implications in what we have done. We still feel obliged to keep feeding Turner's ghost at the table. We may accept the modern view that the West is a settled region distinct unto itself, but we are not always steadfast, clear-minded regionalists in writing its history.

The main questions I now want to raise are these: What is regional history and what is it not? And what strategies should we employ for analyzing this West as region, as opposed to the West as frontier? For the sake of intellectual and moral vitality, regional history should be as inclusive as possible, dealing with anything and everything that has happened to anyone in its territory; it should be total history. Clarifying its purpose should never mean imposing a rigid, doctrinaire formula, especially on so wonderfully diverse a place as the West. But some things are more significant than others in the making of a region. The region has its core influences, just as it has peripheral ones. What we must do is determine what is in that core and what is not.

Begin with what is not. Regional history is not, in the strictest sense, merely the history of the American nation replicating itself, politically, economically, or culturally. Any regional historian must proceed from the assumption that his region is, in some important way, a *unique* part of that greater whole. To find nothing but sameness in it would make his entire enterprise useless. Felix Frankfurter once wrote, "Regionalism is a recognition of the intractable diversities among men, diversities partly shaped by nature but no less derived from the different reactions of men to nature."[9] I will come back to the complicated role of nature in a moment, but for now let us concentrate on that word diversity. The regional historian must be out looking earnestly for it, even when it's hard to find or define, even when it's hard to feel good about when located. But do we do this? Not systematically enough. In fact, one school of thought denies that there has been anything unique or innovative about the West to discover.

Such was the position taken by Earl Pomeroy in 1955, when, in another heroic effort to free us from the influence of Turner, he wrote that "the Westerner has been fundamentally imitator rather than innovator."[10] By example after example, ranging from architecture to territorial government, Pomeroy showed how people in the West drew on the East for their ideas and institutions. To a point he was right, and the argument long overdue. But carry his argument too far and the objection must be raised, why then study the West at all? Why bother with uncovering more and more examples — with mere copies of the original? Better to examine the original itself. If we insist too strenuously that the West has been merely a borrower from the East, it becomes not a region but a province, a dull little backwater of conformists and copycats, all looking to some eastern capital for their inspiration. Nothing would be more tiresome to an active mind than to dwell year after year in such a place. The more ambitious would quickly go elsewhere. Pomeroy certainly did not want that to happen; indeed, he warned the field against slipping into intellectual mediocrity. Yet too much emphasis on the West as continuity would certainly lead us straight to mediocrity and boredom.

Pomeroy properly admonished us against the excesses of exceptionalism. It can lead to extravagant claims of originality, a bumptious chauvinism, a sagebrush rebellion against "outside interference." It can conceal the crucial formative role the federal government has played in the region, particularly through its evolving territorial system, as both Pomeroy and Lamar have shown.[11] But, finally, regionalism is about telling differences or it has nothing to tell.

Nor should regional history be confused, as it sometimes is, with the history of ethnic groups migrating into a place and taking up residence. In fact, I will venture to say that ethnic history and regional history are often conflicting endeavors. In America, ethnic history commonly deals with those "intractable diversities" that have been introduced into this country from abroad and their struggle to survive in the face of pressures to assimilate. Whereas in Europe an ethnic group usually had a regional base — that is, was rooted in a specific geographical place — in the United States it became a moveable identity: a language, some music, holidays and foods, religion, all journeying through space, to a steel town, the prairie, suburbia, yet marvelously remaining intact. Many ethnic groups have come to live in the American West, of course, but the fact of their being in the West is not necessarily the same as their being *of* the West. The ethnic group becomes central to the region's history when and where and to the extent it becomes altered by that region, or develops an active voice in defining the region's "intractable diversity."[12]

Quite different from ethnic history, and presenting an even more intricate problem of fit, is the history of the indigenous peoples who have been invaded and conquered, in this case the Indians and, more ambiguously, the Hispanics. To a greater extent than anyone else, by the fact of their much longer occupation and engagement with the environment, they belong. They are not immigrants, they are natives. But for all that, they are not to be readily or casually absorbed into the study of region. They are sovereign nations that have been unwillingly regionalized — made a part of the "West" (also of the "South" and "Northeast," but especially of the "West") as they have been made by force a part of America. The regionalist who does not begin with their story, their interaction with the place, continues the injustice of their expropriation. But inclusion alone will not do; it is not adequate now merely to make them regional Americans.

Finally, in a mood of rigorous clarification, we must caution that regional history is not quite the same thing as the history of the American or world economic system and their hierarchies of superior and subordinate parts. The western terrain has again and again come under the thumb of some eastern entrepreneur. As William Robbins has recently argued, we need to develop "a broad theoretical formulation that examines the West in the context of its national and international relations" in order to understand that outside exploitation.[13] Quite so, and we ought to ask where all the region's coal, gold, uranium, and timber have gone, and who has profited from them, ask how they have helped build a system of industrial capitalism. But one must be careful not to simply substitute that investigation of outside exploitation for a more complex inquiry into regionalism and its tensions.

The region, the nation, the world: all three are terms in this historical equation, all interacting through time, continually shifting in weight and value, and the regional historian, though committed mainly to understanding the first of them, must not ignore the others. His special task is to understand how those outside economic and political forces, empire and capital, have entered the West and dealt with its regional peculiarities, either by trying to stamp them out or by becoming themselves transformed into new, more indigenous forms.

Those are some of the things, it seems to me, that lie on the periphery, or pose as potential traps, to regional history. What then lies in that core history of the West? What forces and events are to be found there? Recurring to Frankfurter's words, it is the story of the West as one of those intractable diversities which have been "partly shaped by nature but no less derived from the different reactions of men to nature." In other words, the history of the region is first and foremost one of an evolving human ecology. A region emerges as people try to make a living from a particular part of the earth, as they adapt themselves to its limits and possibilities. What the regional historian should first want to know is how a people or peoples acquired a place and, then, how they perceived and tried to make use of it. He will identify the survival techniques they adopted, their patterns of work and economy, and their social relationships.

Put more modishly, the region derives its identity primarily from its ecologically adapted modes of production — or more simply, from its ecological modes.[14] If those modes are precisely the same as those existing elsewhere in the country or world, then we have not got much of a region to study. On the other hand, if the modes are too radically different, we may not have a region at all but rather a foreign civilization. Somewhere between those poles of conformity and differentiation lies the region.

So, leave aside as a related but separate kind of inquiry Merk's wide open frontier, and Turner's process of settlement, and Pomeroy's insistence on continuities. Forget for a while the broader tides of imperialism and Christendom and urbanization and the marketplace. We want to concentrate our attention first on how people have tried to wrest their food, their energy, their income from the specific land in question and what influence that effort has had on the shaping of the West's society and culture.

In our oldest and most distinctive region, the American South, there has been only one dominant ecological mode over most of its history, the plantation system of agriculture in which tobacco and cotton were cultivated by African slave labor. That mode has given the South an enduring identity, a fate that, even now, it has not escaped. More than a hundred years after its defeat in the Civil War, the South can still read its past mode of living in the present condition of its soils, its long backward economic status, and its still troubled racial relations.

In the West, however, we have to deal with not one, but two, primary ecological modes under white occupation. The first of these modes is the life of the cowboy and sheepherder. The second is the life of the irrigator and water engineer. Call these the *pastoral West* and the *hydraulic West.* Neither is found anywhere else in the United States; they are unique to the lands lying beyond Webb and Powell's line of demarcation. What we must understand is how they have evolved side by side, what social impact each has had, where and how they have been in competition with each other, how they have coexisted into our own time, and what cultural values are embedded in each.

All the world knows that the American West is fundamentally a land of cowboys. It is not a myth, however much the fact may have been mythologized in fiction and movies. When the cowboy arrived and commenced punching cows, the West ceased to be a vague frontier of exploration and began, over broad reaches of its territory, in every state from the Great Plains to the Pacific, to take shape as an articulated region.[15]

This West did not develop the way Turner had anticipated. For in his West as process, as social evolution, the pastoral life is supposed to be only a passing stage of settlement and soon must give way to the farmer and the manufacturer. Beyond the hundredth meridian such was not to be the case.

The fur trapper, the miner, and the dirt farmer came to the West, as they did elsewhere on the continent; so too did the missionary and the Indian fighter. All of them had important roles, but none was distinctive to the region, with the possible exception of the hardrock miner. The cowboy, on the other hand, came to stay and built a special way of life.[16] By the early twentieth century that life was firmly rooted in place and being depicted in such works as Wister's *The Virginian* (1902) and Adams's *The Log of a Cowboy* (1903). Even now, in this last quarter of the twentieth century, the pastoral life thrives as well as it ever did. The techniques of range and herd management may have changed, but the basic ecological mode has remained intact. So also endures the cult of self-reliant individualism that has grown up around this mode. We are not in any danger of losing the way of life, nor of missing its historical significance. But even were it to disappear abruptly, it would leave as lasting a mark on the West as the cotton plantation has left on the South.

The hydraulic West, on the other hand, has been much less noticed by western historians.[17] It has taken us by surprise, and we have still not fully comprehended its meaning. This is so for several reasons. The hydraulic West came of age only after World War Two, while western historians have, until late, been preoccupied with the nineteenth century. It is a more technically abstruse and more organizationally complex mode than ranching, therefore requires more effort to penetrate. And, although it has inspired a few songs, movies, and novels, there is too little romance about it to attract popular attention. It is, in fact, too faceless, anonymous, impersonal, even at times too sinister, to be celebrated and loved. This West has been created by irrigation ditches, siphons, canals, and storage dams. In it daily existence depends on the intensive management of that scarce, elusive, and absolutely vital natural resource, water.

The hydraulic mode of living is much older than the grazier's, going back as it does hundreds of years to the Hohokam Indians of Arizona and other native societies.[18] In the modern era of white dominion, the mode first appears in 1847 among the Mormons in their state of Deseret and, soon thereafter, in the Greeley vicinity of Colorado and in California's Central Valley. California would eventually become the principal center of hydraulic development, radiating an influence all the way to Montana and Texas. By 1978, the Census of Agriculture reported 43,668,834 irrigated acres in the seventeen western states: one-tenth of the world's total. California counted 8.6 million acres; Texas, 7 million; Nebraska, 5.7 million; and Idaho and Colorado, 3.5 million each. The market sales from those lands amounted to one-fourth of the nation's total, or $26 billion. Taken by counties, all but one of the top ten agricultural producers in the nation are in the hydraulic West, and eight of them are in California alone.[19]

This water empire is a purely western invention. To be sure, a lot of capital and technology has been invested on farms all over the United States, in the form of machinery, pesticides, fertilizer, and the like; looked at as merely another form of technology, the hydraulic West may appear to be nothing more than an advanced version of modern agribusiness. However, the regional distinctiveness lies in the fact that the typical irrigator is not merely trying to enhance his production by buying a little water now and then. He is critically dependent on that single resource and, to survive, must have it delivered on a steady, reliable basis. There is no room for marketplace competition in his life, no freedom to buy or do without, no substitute available. The western farmer does not have any real choice in the matter; he lives or dies by the level of water in his ditches. This stark fact of utter dependence on an indispensable resource creates a social mode of production.

Given such dependency, the regional historian wants to know what social changes the hydraulic West has worked. How are people organized in this mode? What are their relationships with one another? What qualities of mind and thought appear or take on new emphasis? In what ways does the irrigation infrastructure make this West different from the East or, for that matter, from the pastoral West?

Oddly enough, though he did not think of the West as region, Frederick

Jackson Turner was among the first to discern the peculiar characteristics of this hydraulic life. In an *Atlantic Monthly* article of 1903, he noted that in the preceding fifteen years western settlement had reached the Great Plains, where "new physical conditions have . . . accelerated the social tendency of Western democracy." The conquest of that country would be impossible, he went on, "by the old individual pioneer methods." The new region required "expensive irrigation works," "cooperative activity," and "capital beyond the reach of the small farmer." The condition of water scarcity, he wrote, "decreed that the destiny of this new frontier should be social rather than individual." He compared it to the changes in social structure going on elsewhere in America: this West would be from the outset an "industrial" order, giving rise to "captains of industry," home-grown or imported versions of men like Andrew Carnegie, who were taking charge of the country generally. The task of settling the arid West, like that of creating an industrial society, was too monumental for ordinary people using ordinary skills to carry out; they must therefore "combine under the leadership of the strongest." They would also be forced to rely on the federal government to build for them huge dams and canals as well as show them "what and when and how to plant." "The pioneer of the arid regions," Turner concluded, "must be both a capitalist and the protégé of the government."[20] That these were fundamental differences from the requirements of raising food and fiber in the East, Turner clearly understood, yet strangely he assumed that his vaunted frontier democracy would be unaffected by them. To see matters otherwise would have shattered the hopeful, nationalistic pride he felt in the westward movement. We, on the other hand, can put realistic names to the social conditions emerging in this West: hierarchy, concentration of wealth and power, rule by expertise, dependency on government and bureaucracy. The American deserts could be made to grow some crops all right, but among them would be the crop of oligarchy.

That fact was already faintly discernible eighty-three years ago. By the late 1930s, John Steinbeck could confirm them in his novel, *The Grapes of Wrath,* which portrays the hydraulic West through the eyes of the Joads of Oklahoma. Forced to migrate west, the Joads become members of a permanent underclass of stoop-and-pick laborers, an underclass that had access neither to the land nor the water needed to make it flourish. Steinbeck sensed that there was no simple alternative to that undemocratic outcome, not so long as the West wanted or needed a hydraulic system and wanted it to grow more and more elaborate. Some form of power elite, whether possessing capital, or expertise, or both, would be required to carry out that ambition. It need not be a capitalistic elite that would rise to command. Government could intervene in the outcome, not only to develop more water but also to distribute it into more hands. But in doing so, the government would itself become a form of concentrated power, threatening to dominate people's lives to an often intolerable degree. Quite simply, the domination of nature in the water empire must lead to the domination of some people by others.[21]

Another outcome of the hydraulic mode, likewise unanticipated at the beginning and even now not commonly realized, is an intensification and concentration of urban growth. Cities need water too; and in a region of scarcity, where water sources are few and far between, the city must reach out over great distances to fill that necessity. The bigger the city, the more power it has to wield over its rivals. In this competition, the small community is at a disadvantage, short as it is of both capital and technical virtuosity. Inevitably, it loses out or it becomes a dependent on the metropolis, as the Owens Valley of California has done in its struggle with Los Angeles. Webb noted the outcome of this unequal competition: "The West is today virtually an oasis civilization."[22] Despite an abundance of space, people have found themselves being driven to a few isolated oases where they live packed closely together, while all around them the land stretches away like a great, wild void.

Finally, the hydraulic West has touched and shaped people's imaginations in ways we have hardly yet understood. Old ideas have been reborn there, or they have been applied in new ways. For example, the Americans who came into the region brought with them a deeply rooted drive for mastery over the natural world. They did not come to contemplate the land, nor would they easily tolerate any deprivations it imposed on them. We will make a stand here in this awesome canyon, westerners began to say, and hold back with our common force the full might of the Columbia, the Snake, the Missouri, the Platte, the Rio Grande, the Colorado. No individual or small knot of people among us can achieve that triumph. It will require all of us working as one, all of us united in the pursuit of power. In contrast to the pastoral West, with its glorification of rugged individualism, this hydraulic mode has promoted the cultish idea of the collective domination of nature.[23]

There are many resemblances between this hydraulic West and the modern technological society, as found today in Moscow, New York, or Tokyo. But they are not quite the same thing — not yet anyway. The technological society believes it has escaped all environmental restraint, overcome all limits, and at last stands free of nature. But in today's West such a boast would be ludicrous. The region obviously has not yet learned how to manufacture a single molecule of water, let alone water in unlimited quantities, nor even to find a single substitute for it. Water remains a severely limited resource, yet it is irreplaceable. Until the West discovers how to produce this resource in unstinting abundance, it must continue to obey nature's demands. And in that obedience the West remains a region set apart from other regions.[24]

Through this recapitulation of the two major western modes, I have been indicating a strategy of analysis that, if followed, would take us to the true West at last. Walter Prescott Webb told us where we might find it some time ago, but then he himself got discouraged and turned back. There was not enough intellectual substance along the way, he feared, to satisfy the historian. "Western history," he wrote in his 1957 essay, "is brief and it is bizarre. It is brief because the time is so short and its material deficient. Western history is bizarre because of the nature of what it has got." Having spent some time in England as a visiting professor, having travelled widely around the East and South, he had come home to the West in the fifties with a heightened sense of it as a place "full of negatives and short on positives." Above all, the region's lack of water seemed to him responsible somehow for its failure to achieve a larger cultural significance.

> What is the biographer going to do for a region that has so few men of distinction: What is the historian going to do with a country almost without chronology or important battles or great victories or places where armies have surrendered or dead soldiers were buried? How can he make a thick history out of such thin material? [25]

We have heard such laments before. It is the old, piteous cry of the provincial who has lost confidence in himself and his ability to find complex meaning in his surroundings. Perhaps, to avoid such doubt, the western historian ought to stay away from places like Oxford. Or if he insists on visiting them, he ought to remind himself that, looked at up close, their old kings and warriors were not any better than the new ones; that, anyway, battles and armies are not the only stuff of history. He ought to read and reread as often as possible what Ortega y Gasset once wrote, that arid lands do not necessarily make arid minds. [26] But Webb forgot all that. Late in his life he seems to have lost enthusiasm for the West as region and instead began denigrating it. Now it falls to a later generation — our generation — to push ahead toward a deeper, fuller, and more intellectually complex regionalism.

If Clifford Geertz can find large meanings in the cockfights of Bali and Emmanuel Le Roy Ladurie in the peasants of Languedoc, the western historian need not despair of the West. [27] For those with imagination to find it, there is plenty of thick history to be written about this region. Within its spacious boundaries and across its spare, dry expanses, through what is now more than two hundred years of European settlement and many thousand of Indian life, this region offers for study all the greed, violence, beauty, ambition, and variety anyone could use. Given enough time and effort, it may someday also offer a story of careful, lasting adaptation of people to the land.

We are beginning to know where the true West is, what it has been, what it might have been, what it might still be. We are beginning to know the place for the first time.

Notes

1. Howard Lamar, ed., *The Reader's Encyclopedia of the American West* (New York, 1977), 710–12.

2. Frederick Merk, *History of the Westward Movement* (New York, 1978), 616–17.

3. Ray Allen Billington, *Westward Expansion: A History of the American Frontier,* 4th ed., (New York, 1974), 29, 648.

4. Turner to Merle Curti, cit., Wilbur Jacobs, "Frederick Jackson Turner," in *Turner, Bolton, and Webb: Three Historians of the American Frontier* (Seattle, 1965), 8.

5. Ibid., 9. I am aware that Turner also contributed much to our thinking about sections and regions in American history. On this subject, see Michael C. Steiner, "The Significance of Turner's Sectional Thesis," *Western Historical Quarterly,* 10 (October 1979), 437–66. Turner did not, however, see "the West" as a cohesive whole, fixed in place. He divided the country into eight regions: New England, the Middle States, the Southeast, the Southwest, the Middle West, the Great Plains, the Mountain States, and the Pacific Coast. (Turner, "Sections and Nation," *Yale Review,* 12 [October 1922], 2.)

6. Walter Prescott Webb, "The American West: Perpetual Mirage," *Harper's Magazine,* 214 (May 1957), 25. See also James Malin, "Webb and Regionalism," in *History and Ecology: Studies of the Grassland,* ed. Robert Swierenga (Lincoln, 1984), 85–104.

7. Powell used Charles Shott's "Rain Chart of the United States" to delineate the Arid Region. Shott's twenty-inch isohyet actually corresponds to the hundredth meridian only in Texas and the Indian Territory (Oklahoma); then it veers slightly eastward to include all of the Dakotas and the northwestern corner of Minnesota. The western edge of the region excludes all of northern California, the Sierra Nevada, and western Oregon and Washington — following roughly the one-hundred twentieth meridian north of Reno. The whole embraced almost half of the United States outside Alaska. See J. W. Powell, *Report on the Lands of the Arid Region,* 45th Cong. 2nd sess., House Executive Document 73 (Washington, D.C., 1878), see map included.

8. *Historians and the American West,* ed. Michael Malone (Lincoln, 1983), 2.

9. Felix Frankfurter, cit., in Merrill Jensen, ed., *Regionalism in America* (Madison, 1951), xvi. An excellent recent essay on regionalism, with ample bibliography, is Richard Maxwell Brown's "The New Regionalism in America, 1970–1981," in William G. Robbins, Robert J. Frank, and Richard E. Ross, eds., *Regionalism and the Pacific Northwest* (Corvallis, 1983), 37–96.

10. Earl Pomeroy, "Toward a Reorientation of Western History: Continuity and Environment," *Mississippi Valley Historical Review,* 41 (March 1955), 581–82. Pomeroy also rejected the claim that their environment made westerners more radical than other Americans, a point he wins hands down.

11. See Earl Pomeroy, *The Territories and the United States, 1861–1912: A Territorial History* (New Haven, 1966).

12. The most thoughtful student of the relation between ethnicity and region has been Frederick C. Luebke. See his "Ethnic Minority Groups in the American West," in Malone, *Historians and the American West,* 387–413; and also his "Regional-

ism and the Great Plains: Problems of Concept and Method," *Western Historical Quarterly,* 15 (January 1984), 19–38.

13. William G. Robbins, "The 'Plundered Province' Thesis and the Recent Historiography of the American West," *Pacific Historical Review,* 55 (November 1986), 577–97.

14. The phrase "mode of production" has its origins in Marxist scholarship, where it refers to both technology ("forces") and social or class relations. See, among other works, Barry Hindess and Paul Q. Hirst, *Pre-capitalist Modes of Production* (London, 1975), 9–12; James F. Becker, *Marxian Political Economy: An Outline* (Cambridge, 1977), 35; Aidan Foster-Carter, "The Modes of Production Controversy," *New Left Review,* 107 (January-February 1978), 47–78. Here, I use the phrase more loosely, and with revision, to indicate, first, a set of techniques adapted for the exploitation of particular environments and, second, a resulting social organization.

15. The origins of the western cattle industry have recently been traced to the Old South by geographer Terry Jordan in *Trails to Texas: Southern Roots of Western Cattle Ranching* (Lincoln, 1981). Whatever its source, the pastoral mode became, for ecological and economic reasons, ultimately rooted in the West.

16. Gilbert Fite has reviewed some of the major titles on this subject in Malone, *Historians and the American West,* 221–24 and 230–33. What is so far missing from any of the literature on American pastoralism is any awareness that this mode has expressions all over the world, has been well studied by anthropologists, and needs some comparative and cross-disciplinary work by historians. See, for example, Walter Goldschmidt, "A General Model for Pastoral Social Systems," *Pastoral Production and Society* (Cambridge, 1979), 15–27; Brian Spooner, *The Cultural Ecology of Pastoral Nomads,* Addison-Wesley Module in Anthropology No. 45 (Reading, Mass., 1973); Z. A. Konczacki, *The Economics of Pastoralism: A Case Study of Sub-Saharan Africa* (London, 1978); John Galaty et al., *The Future of Pastoral Peoples: Proceedings of a Conference held in Nairobi, Kenya, 4 August 1980* (Ottawa, 1981); and the classic study by E. E. Evans Pritchard, *The Nuer, a Description of the Modes of Livelihood and Political Institutions of a Nilotic People* (Oxford, 1940).

17. Notable exceptions to this observation include such works as Norris Hundley, *Water and the West: The Colorado River Compact and the Politics of Water in the American West* (Berkeley, 1975); Lawrence Lee, *Reclaiming the American West: An Historiography and Guide* (Santa Barbara, 1980); William Kahrl, *Water and Power: The Conflict Over Los Angeles' Water Supply in the Owens Valley* (Berkeley, 1982); Donald J. Pisani, *From the Family Farm to Agribusiness: The Irrigation Crusade in California, 1850–1930* (Berkeley, 1984); and Robert G. Dunbar, *Forging New Rights in Western Waters* (Lincoln, 1983).

18. See, for example, Emil Haury, *The Hohokam, Desert Farmers and Craftsmen: Excavations at Snaketown, 1964–1965* (Tucson, 1976); and, for even more ancient examples, Karl Wittfogel, *Oriental Despotism: A Comparative Study of Total Power* (New Haven, 1957); Anne Bailey and Josep Llobers, eds., *The Asiatic Mode of Production* (London, 1981); Julian Steward, ed., *Irrigation Civilizations* (Washington, D.C., 1955).

19. U.S. Department of Commerce, *1978 Census of Agriculture. Vol. 4, Irrigation* (Washington, D.C., 1982), 30. Council for Agricultural Science and Technology, *Water Use in Agriculture: Now and For the Future,* Report No. 95 (September 1982), 13.

20. Frederick Jackson Turner, "Contributions of the West to American Democracy," and "Pioneer Ideals," reprinted in his collected essays, *The Frontier in American History* (New York, 1920), 258–59, 278–79.

21. My own book, *Rivers of Empire: Water, Aridity, and the Growth of the American West* (New York, 1985), is an attempt to reinterpret the West as a modern hydraulic society. I discuss Steinbeck's California on pp. 213–33.

22. Webb, "The American West," 28. See also Gerald Nash, *The American West in the Twentieth Century: A Short History of an Urban Oasis* (Englewood Cliffs, 1973), 5; and Earl Pomeroy, *The Pacific Slope: A History of California, Oregon, Washington, Idaho, Utah, and Nevada* (New York, 1965).

23. For the larger dimensions of this idea see William Leiss, *The Domination of Nature* (New York, 1972); and Michael Zimmerman, "Marx and Heidegger on the Technological Domination of Nature," *Philosophy Today*, 23 (1979), 99–112.

24. It might be argued that, even in the global technological society, there are and always will be regional differences — that in its triumph over nature, technology still bears the imprint of what it has conquered. But for most people the experience of living in advanced technological systems is that they lose any sense of regional uniqueness.

25. Webb, "The American West," 29, 31.

26. Ortega y Gasset, "Arid Plains, and Arid Men," in *Invertebrate Spain*, trans. Mildred Adams (New York, 1937), 158–65.

27. Clifford Geertz, *The Interpretation of Cultures: Selected Essays* (New York, 1977), Chap. 15; and Emmanuel Le Roy Ladurie, *The Peasants of Languedoc*, trans. John Day (Urbana, 1974).

6. How should we interpret the frontier / West?

Patricia Nelson Limerick, Michael P. Malone, Gerald Thompson, and Elliott West

Western History: Why the Past May Be Changing

These four brief essays provide a revealing glimpse of recent differences dividing historians writing about the frontier and the American West. The four authors were asked to examine the meaning of the New Western history and to assess its impact on recent historical writing about the American West. Taken together, these essays furnish students with an illuminating example of what historians call "historiography," the varying viewpoints of scholars about a subject of history.

Patricia Nelson Limerick, professor of history at the University of Colorado, Boulder, is widely known as the leading New Western historian. Here, in the best brief discussion of the central ideas of this movement, she describes the New Western history as more realistic, complex, and multicultural than Turnerian views of the frontier. Limerick also stresses continuity between the American West of the pre- and post-1900 periods and calls for interpretations less tied to the romantic, exceptionalist views of Turner.

Michael P. Malone, a well-known western historian and the president of Montana State University, is less convinced that a New Western history has emerged. Yet Malone agrees that notable changes in the past generation have transformed historical writing about the West. Rather than castigate earlier Turnerian views, Malone calls for a new way of viewing the West, a "regional paradigm [that] must be multifaceted." If historians become less tied to a frontier past and instead approach the American West as a dynamic, evolving frontier, Malone adds, they will meet the challenge of a more realistic, useful historiography.

Gerald Thompson, now deceased, was professor of history at the University of Toledo and the editor of *The Historian*. His essay discusses the difficulties and challenges of frontier and regional interpretations of the American West. Yet Thompson is less critical of the frontier past than is Limerick or other New Western historians. Drawing on student answers to the question "What comes to mind when you think of the West?" he urges historians to consider the West as both frontier process and evolving region.

Elliott West, professor of history at the University of Arkansas, disagrees with Malone and Thompson and agrees with Limerick. There is a New Western history, West asserts, and it has accomplished a great deal. These newer historians treat the American West in a larger national, even global, perspective. The New Westerners, by examining the daily lives of all western residents, also provide a fuller, richer portrait of the West. True, the story may be grimmer and more messy, but West is convinced that western historians and novelists alike are now providing the kinds of complex, realistic narratives of the western past we have always needed.

Questions for a Closer Reading

1. Judging from these four historiographical arguments, how would you define the New Western history, and how does it differ from Turner's ideas of the frontier and American exceptionalism?

2. Which of these essays do you find the most persuasive? Why?

3. How would you distinguish between the frontier as process and the West as region?

4. Limerick and West are less positive than Malone and Thompson about the frontier past. Do you find yourself

agreeing or disagreeing with this more pessimistic view ? Why or why not?

5. Which of these essayists most closely approximates your own view of the frontier and the West? How so?

Western History: Why the Past May Be Changing

What follows are essays by four leading scholars of western history who were asked to consider what the "new western history" is, exactly, what its impact on western history has been thus far, and where it might lead as we move into the 1990s and beyond. The authors, Patricia Nelson Limerick, Michael P. Malone, Gerald Thompson, and Elliott West, provide a range of views that might help clarify what is happening to western history.

One thing is clear. As these four essays show, there is the constructive tension of dissent, disagreement, and ferment. The old and familiar are being assessed anew, while new and different horizons are being explored in all directions. As some scholars re-evaluate the eighteenth- and nineteenth-century western experience, others lay the foundations for understanding the twentieth-century West.

The influence of perspectives originating in the 1960s is unmistakable. The new emphasis on historical ethnic and racial diversity, for example, not only reflects the rejection of melting pot homogeneity but represents the logical extension of notions of social and cultural pluralism that first emerged in the decade of Kennedy and Johnson. Similarly, the new emphasis on man's historic interaction with the environment follows on the concern for ecological fragility and environmental exploitation that first emerged in its contemporary form a quarter century ago. Likewise, the explosion of work in western women's history, which began in the 1970s and

"Western History: Why the Past May Be Changing," *Montana: The Magazine of Western History* 40 (Summer 1990): 60–76.

gained increasing momentum in the 1980s, can be linked to feminism's insistence in the late 1960s that women be recognized as active players in all facets of society.

Consider the results. Women have become an essential part of the western story, as have ethnic and racial groups. Viewing the past from their perspectives, we find cultural and social complexity in place of archetypal male simplicity. Rather than seeing a single Anglo wave moving westward across a continent, we see one wave, predominantly but not wholly Anglo, encountering other waves, one Hispanic from the south, another Asian from the Far West, and amidst it all, we find enduring yet dynamic Native American cultures. The environment is no longer a barrier to be overcome, but a vital historical component that itself changes with human interaction even as it shapes western economic and social patterns, not to mention the imagination.

Perhaps most importantly, the new western history offers a more balanced view of the western past. It includes failure as well as success; defeat as well as victory; sympathy, grace, villainy, and despair as well as daring, courage, and heroism; women as well as men; varied ethnic groups and their differing perspectives as well as white Anglo-Saxon Protestants; an environment that is limiting, interactive, and sometimes ruined as well as mastered and made to bloom; a parochial economy alternately fueled and abandoned by an interlocking national and world order; and, finally, a regional identity as well as a frontier ethic.

Frederick Jackson Turner, father of the frontier thesis, comes in for hard criticism for having bequeathed what many historians regard as an interpretive straightjacket. We should remember not only that Turner was a man of his times, however, but that he realized that fact. It was Turner, after all, who said that each generation interprets history anew, according to its own need for understanding. History thus can never be static, set down once and for all. One of history's highest goals is to make the past useable. If the new western history does nothing else, it helps us consider the old and familiar in new ways. And if we are fortunate, these new perspectives will be relevant to our times.

What on Earth Is the New Western History?

BY PATRICIA NELSON LIMERICK

I am from Banning, California, a town on the edge of the desert, eighty miles southeast of Los Angeles. When I grew up there, cattle grazed at the Brinton Ranch north of town, and once a year we celebrated Stagecoach Days, commemorating Banning's location on a principal route of travel into coastal California through the San Gorgonio Pass. Forest fires sometimes consumed the mountains on either side of the pass; I remember Mt. San Jacinto in flames, with the sky glowing in that weird way that only a forest fire produces.

Banning was, from its aridity to its mountain setting, a world apart from Portage, Wisconsin, the hometown of Frederick Jackson Turner. Turner grew up in a place with plenty of water, a place remote from the Pacific Coast and the Mexican border. Indian people, French Canadians, and a variety of people of northern European background played their role in the area's history. But on this count, too, Banning was a world apart — with Cahuilla Indians from the Morongo Reservation on the edge of town; Hispanic people of varying origins — longterm residents of the United States as well as more recent immigrants; Afro-Americans; Filipinos; and "white" people, with all the range of backgrounds that that odd category carries.

There has been a grand tradition in western American history, a tradition in which I am proud to play a small part, of taking one's home seriously. Turner took Portage seriously; Walter Prescott Webb took his Texas plains home seriously; and after a spell of wondering why I had to grow up in a town that seemed so far from the main course of American history, I ended up taking Banning seriously.

Take Banning seriously, and you find yourself immediately in the role of rebel against the standing models of western history. Tailored to fit Portage, Wisconsin, Turner's frontier theory simply won't fit Banning, regardless of how you trim and stitch, tighten and loosen. Western American historians with backgrounds like my own had the choice of accepting the standard, Turner-derived interpretations of the field and discarding our own personal experience or trusting our experience and discarding the old theories. It is a tribute to the power of tradition that so many western historians submitted to the first option so long and chose theory over experience.

Conventional frontier theory never made much room for the West beyond the hundredth meridian. Any number of central characteristics of that region played either a limited role, or no role at all in Turner's thinking. Western aridity is only the most obvious. The continued presence and resistance to conquest of Indian people; Spanish settlement in the Southwest preceding Anglo-American settlement anywhere in North America as well as the continued give-and-take between Latin America and Anglo America; the industrial reality of much western mining; Asian immigration and the West's involvement in the Pacific Rim; ongoing disputes over the ownership and management of public lands; the existence of something other than the ideal pioneer democracy and equality in western state and local governments — most of these central items found their homes on the edges of the field, if they found any home at all.

Just as important as Turner's lack of attention to the Far West was the accumulation of a century's worth of history since he made his major statement on the meaning of the frontier. A man of considerable intellectual courage, Turner said that the frontier ended in 1890, and he made this claim a bare three years after 1890. In this willingness to assess the currents of his own time, Turner was virtually kin to the John Naisbitts and Alvin Tofflers* of our own time, standing on the edge of the future and forecasting megatrends.

Courageous certainly, Turner was also, on this count, wrong. If the "frontier" meant, in one of its many and changeable definitions, the discovery of new resources and the rush of population to exploit those resources, then 1890 was no deadline. Homesteading persisted into the twentieth century; rushes to pump oil, or to mine coal or uranium, punctuated the 1900s. In sheer numbers, the westward movement of the twentieth century far outweighed the westward movement of the nineteenth century. Moreover, the cross-cultural encounters and conflicts engendered by the "frontier" are still with us in 1990; the population of western America shows few signs of turning into a blended and homogeneous whole.

Personal experience had taught me a great deal of this long before I had any professional interest in western American history. In the 1940s, in the process of moving from Los Angeles to Banning, my parents had given my older sister, Ingrid, an early and perhaps excessive exposure to the language of that archetypal figure of western expansion, the real estate agent. On one outing, Ingrid woke up from a nap in the backseat of the car, looked out the window, and asked where she was. "In Temecula," was the answer, and Ingrid then solemnly declared: "I think Temecula is going to grow and grow and grow."

In my own childhood, we laughed at this story because Temecula did not grow. But then, in the 1970s, my sister's long-term gift of prophecy became clear. Temecula grew and grew and grew, and we stopped laughing and started wondering why Mother and Father hadn't had the sense to borrow money and *buy* Temecula in 1950. But encased in this piece of family folklore was an essential message about the unpredictability of western American life and about the folly of believing that any "end of the frontier" had put to rest these matters of regional growth and instability.

By the 1980s, the field of western American history was ripe for major change. Not only was there evidence, in Temecula and elsewhere, that life in the region had not settled into a post-frontier sameness, there was also a

---

Alvin Toffler and John Naisbitt: Two authors who became well known for predicting future trends in the United States and around the globe: Toffler, *Future Shock* (1970), and Naisbitt, *Megatrends* (1982).

wonderful accumulation of innovative, scholarly books in the fields of environmental, ethnic, community, and women's history as well as social, economic, and political history. Much of the content of those books strains the limits of Turnerian frontier models; indeed, by the early 1980s, it seemed to me that the accumulation of new studies had burst through those limits entirely. But we had no book reuniting these scattered subfields into one whole model.

It was my enormous good fortune to be seized by a spirit of daring and, under its influence, to resolve to write a book offering a new synthesis. Writing such a book offers the author opportunities to feel deep and compelling anxiety. For virtually every paragraph, the writer recognizes five or ten experts who know the subject in considerably greater depth than any synthesizer possibly could. But each of those moments of high anxiety is counterbalanced by much longer spells of excitement and satisfaction. Writing *The Legacy of Conquest,* I was in daily, face-to-face contact with the breadth, drama, and power of western American history, even when I was not entirely succeeding in capturing those qualities in prose.

Published in 1987, *The Legacy of Conquest* has had a remarkably happy career, passionately loved by some, passionately hated by others, and creatively revised and responded to by many more. Publishing a book can sometimes feel like shouting in a fully soundproofed room, but *Legacy* has been heard in a way that has exceeded my wildest dreams, back in Banning, that I might someday be an author.

What, then, is the essence of this emerging way of looking at the western past? Preparing for a symposium called "Trails: Toward a New Western History" (held in Santa Fe, New Mexico, in September 1989), one of the participants quite sensibly wrote me to ask what this phrase "new western history" meant. In response, I wrote a summation, a one-page text that has had a prosperous career in copying machines and appears here in print for the first time:

New Western historians define "the West" primarily as a place — the trans-Mississippi region in the broadest terms, or the region west of the hundredth meridian. The boundaries are fuzzy because nearly all regional boundaries are.

New western historians do see a "process" at work in this region's history, a process that has affected other parts of the nation as well as other parts of the planet. But they reject the old term "frontier" for that process. When clearly and precisely defined, the term "frontier" is nationalistic and often racist (in essence, the area where white people get scarce); when cleared of its ethnocentrism, the term loses an exact definition.

To characterize the process that shaped the region, new western historians have available a number of terms — invasion, conquest, colonization, exploitation, development, expansion of the world market. In the broadest picture, the process involves the convergence of diverse people — women as well as men, Indians, Europeans, Latin Americans, Asians, Afro-Americans — in the region, and their encounters with each other and with the natural environment.

New western historians reject the notion of a clear-cut "end to the frontier" in 1890, or in any other year. The story of the region's sometimes contested, sometimes cooperative relations among its diverse cast of characters and the story of human efforts to "master" nature in the region, are both ongoing stories, with their continuity unnecessarily ruptured by attempts to divide the "old West"" from the "new West."

New western historians break free of the old model of "progress" and "improvement," and face up to the possibility that some roads of western development led directly to failure and to injury. This reappraisal is not meant to make white Americans "look bad." The intention is, on the contrary, simply to make it clear that in western American history, heroism and villany, virtue and vice, nobility and shoddiness appear in roughly the same proportions as they appear in any other subject of human history (and with the same relativity of definition and judgment). This is only disillusioning to those who have come to depend on illusions.

New western historians surrender the conventional, never-very-convincing claim of an omniscient, neutral objectivity. While making every effort to acknowledge and understand different points of view, new western historians admit that it is OK for scholars to care about their subjects, both in the past and the present, and to put that concern on record.

Does all this add up to a revolution that should alarm westerners outside the ivory towers? A grumpy columnist for the *Arizona Republic* (October 23, 1989, p. A10), responding to news of the "Trails" conference, seemed to think so: "Why can't the revisionists simply leave our myths alone?" Phil Sunkel wrote. "Westerners — and most other Americans, for that matter — are quite content with our storied past, even if it tends to fib a bit." To this writer and others of his persuasion, the western public is composed of cheerful fools, people happy to deny their own lived experience out of a preference for appealing and colorful legends.

My own experience, speaking to diverse public audiences around the West, leads to very different conclusions. Far from a region filled with Hollywood's dupes and suckers, the American West in 1990 has a population well-supplied with serious, concerned citizens, people doing the best they can to figure out where they are and who they are. These people are usually quick to accept the new western history. It takes the region, its dilemmas and its charms, seriously; it restores full human dignity to westerners of the past and present; by dissolving the great divide between the "old West" and the "new West," it simply does a better job of explaining how we got to where we are today. We cannot take ourselves and our present challenges seriously, many westerners realize, until we take our history seriously. We cannot live responsibly in the American West until we have made a responsible and thorough assessment of our common past.

This is not, by any means, to say that audiences shift immediately into full, unquestioning acceptance of the new approach. The new western history is not a party line; it is not a set of principles to which all members must swear allegiance. It is, instead, a movement to allow westerners to take their home towns seriously, to let Banning, California, stand up to the previous dominance of Portage, Wisconsin. But the most fundamental mission of the new western history is to widen the range and increase the vitality of the search for meaning in the western past. Thanks to its critics and opponents, as well as to its supporters and advocates, that mission has been accomplished.

The "New Western History": An Assessment

BY MICHAEL P. MALONE

A friend of mine who is a theologian once said that his is the only discipline in which the very existence of the subject matter is open to dispute. Similarly, it is truly questionable whether there is a "new western history."

In the sense of a genuinely defined school of interpretation, there is probably not. The new western history can claim no precise definition to match that of the revisionist school of diplomatic history introduced by William Appleman Williams and others three decades ago, nor even as much precision as that claimed by the celebrated *Annales* group of "nonevent-oriented" history. In fact, it would seem to lack even the coherence of that generation of American historians who, three-quarters of a century ago, called for a "new" or "progressive" orientation toward the study of the past.

Yet, in broader perspective, the main currents of western historiography have shifted remarkably both in direction and in velocity during the past two decades and especially in the past few years. It seems warranted, therefore, to conclude that, while there is no narrowly defined school of new western history, there is indeed a broad reconfiguration of this subdiscipline of American history emerging that might be so labeled. The correct question then becomes: what is the nature of this reconfiguration?

This question begs another: What is the "older western history"? That one is easy enough to answer. The traditional western history is essentially frontier history, focusing upon a *to-the-region* approach and featuring a heavily romanticized preoccupation with wilderness, Indians and pioneers, and the adventure of conquering one new land after another.

As most everyone knows, the conceptual lodestone of this frontier/western historiography was provided by Frederick Jackson Turner, who began in the 1890s to describe the frontier experience as the forge of American national identity and the font of such enduring national traits as individualism and democracy. Turner was not a historian of the West but of the frontier. Arguably, the greatest of the true western regionalists was the Texas historian Walter Prescott Webb, who saw in the abiding aridity of the West the main shaping force of its regional identity. But Webb, too, preoccupied himself with frontiering, and his writings reinforce the Turnerian/frontier bent of western studies rather than challenge it.

Thus, the classic paradigm of western history emphasized the frontier, the Americanization of the land and its peoples, and the early eras of land- and resource-taking. Conversely, of course, it neglected the post-frontier eras that followed the 1890s, the diversity of peoples outside the Anglo/white mainstream, and the women and children who less frequently wielded rifles, plows, and axes. Also neglected were the cities with their industries, professions, and life experiences that seemed alien to an agrarian frontier even when cities arose in the west before farm economies.

On the one hand, western history's preoccupation with the frontier has produced some of the best narrative writings in all of Americana, from Francis Parkman to Bernard DeVoto and Robert Utley. Historians of the West have held the popular audiences that most of their colleagues have lost. This important fact should not be disregarded, nor should the ever greater numbers of excellent and sophisticated frontier histories that appear yearly. But the truth is inescapable that preoccupation with the frontier in western history has tended over the years to stigmatize it as romantic, antiquarian, and — worst of all — irrelevant to achieving a true regionalism.

Whether we choose to call the remarkable enrichment of the field during the past quarter-century a new western history or not, the fact is that the timeworn themes and preoccupations of the old West have been visibly crumbling recently in the face of an unprecedented surge of scholarly vitality. In large part, this surge is simply the predictable result of mainstreaming the western subdiscipline by the application to it of trends in the broader field of American history and American studies.

A closer look tends to reinforce this judgment, for the main thrusts of the new western history are generally those of modern American historiography itself. The remarkable increase in attention to western women, for example, led by historians like Julie Roy Jeffrey, Sandra Myres, and Glenda Riley, is now joined by dozens of others. Another example is the ever greater attention Francis Paul Prucha, Lawrence Kelly, and others are paying to western Indians and Indian policy and to other regional minorities as well, particularly Hispanics and Asians. Still other examples include the new urban history of the West, particularly the Southwest; the profusion of writings about all aspects of the western environment; and the increasing application of quantification and the new social history to western topics.

Conversely, the new western history has had the least impact in precisely those areas of emphasis that the new American historiography itself has slighted, namely the prosaic but fundamental mainstays of human activity and history — the economy, the political-governmental order, and the major events of day-to-day life. Consequently, as the newer western history tends to be less political and economic and more socially oriented, it runs the risk of losing its relevance and appeal to the broader literate public. This is what has happened to the wider field of history in general.

The subfield of the West still maintains its distinctiveness within the larger field of American history, however, as a visit to any annual conference of the Western History Association quickly makes clear. This distinctiveness serves to remind us that there is more to the new western history than simply the regional application of national trends. The West as a field of Americana still appeals to the broader public, not just because of the frontier mystique, but also because of the public's fascination with the West as a place, a unique place. The most subtle challenge to contemporary historians of the West is to make the field relevant while not losing the attention of the literate public.

To do so, they must not only maintain the humanism and attention to well-crafted narrative that comprise the essence of any truly societally based history. They must also join in the search for a new paradigm upon which to base a genuine regionalism. Without such a reconceptualization, historians of the West must either continue to follow the threadbare environmental determinisms of Turner and Webb, or follow the unrewarding practice of simply interpreting national events and trends in unexplored regional settings.

During the past decade, historians of the West have made considerable progress along new lines of thought. Some of the most thoughtful of them, particularly historians of cities, women, and minorities, have simply dismissed the older approach of Turner and Webb as irrelevant, or at least outmoded, and moved on to address their subjects in the best ways possible. Earl Pomeroy, the dean of western historians, for example, has discarded the frontier orientation in favor of an interpretation that stresses continuity of development and the role of cities. Pomeroy also eschews the lively narrative in favor of close analysis.

However much the new regional history accomplishes through scholarship that broadens and deepens the field, it still must come to terms with the search for regional identity. Once it does so, the old problem of dual identity between college courses on the frontier and those on the West will fade. Frontier, or *to-the-West* courses will still be taught, but they won't be confused with *in-the-region* courses that are the natural counterparts of regional offerings on the South, New England, or the Midwest, or of courses that address similar global regions such as the Russian steppes or the African savannahs.

To my mind, the most interesting facet of current western historiography is this search for a post-Turnerian paradigm for regional study. Three scholars associated with the Yale University doctoral program in western studies — a program so prolific that some consider it to *be* the new western history — offer three separate approaches to this end.

Patricia Nelson Limerick, for one, attempts to establish a "legacy of conquest" to replace the Turnerian frontier approach. While stimulating, her interpretation seems not really to address the West as place. William Cronon ingeniously argues that the new environmental history is the natural modernization of Turner's environmental interpretation. And Donald Worster argues, quite convincingly, that the true essence of western history is, as Webb said, its aridity and basic reliance upon fragile water systems.

Personally, I believe that the new regional paradigm must be multi-faceted, not singular. The enduring impact of both Turner's frontier and Webb's aridity must be taken into account. Equally important, however, are other regionally binding factors such as the federal presence in the region, the special importance of extractive industries, and the ongoing process of integrating the West into the global economy. This latter process is one in which the resource-reliant West lies on the cutting edge of America's ongoing factoring into what Immanuel Wallerstein calls the "world-system."

Thus, the search for a new regional paradigm need not mean an outright rejection of Turner and Webb's frontier preoccupation, but it certainly does require a broadening and enrichment of a focus that by itself is too narrow. This is clearly happening. Whether or not one chooses to term this flowering of regional writing a new western history, it is truly the birth of an authentic *regional* historiography, and the phenomenon is indisputably genuine. Out of the current multiplicity of gender and ethnic studies; community and city histories; and economic, policy, and political histories, I hope will emerge our first real comprehension of the West-as-region. That will be something to celebrate.

Another Look at Frontier versus Western Historiography

BY GERALD THOMPSON

Have you ever noticed that in almost every book or article written about the frontier or the West the authors invariably fail to define these two most essential terms? A recent notable exception was Patricia Nelson Limerick's *Legacy of Conquest* (1987), which argued that the word *frontier* should be read as *conquest.* Her book and the response to it indicate that historians still cannot define their terms in a very satisfying manner.

Brave historians like Limerick step forward occasionally and attempt definition, but due to a simplicity of analysis, or perhaps a faulty paradigm, the new western historians have presented an easy target for their intellectual opponents. When Donald Worster asserted that the arid West was the true West, the printer's ink hardly had dried on his article before critics noted the *arid* definition excluded the Pacific Northwest, northern California, parts of the Rocky Mountains, and the eastern half of the Great Plains.[1]

The efforts of other scholars have proved about as successful, or unsuccessful, as Limerick's and Worster's. Gerald Nash declared the western region a spiritual place rather than *terra firma.* But if we adopt Nash's spiritual boundaries of the region, what do we do with those geographical realities of Arizona, Nebraska, and Montana?[2] In an article appearing in this magazine, Charles S. Peterson tackled the question in a slightly different form, asking "What is Western History?" Peterson concluded that the status of western history reminded him of the parable of the blind men and the elephant. Each historian grasps a part of the great beast, but each lacks the vision to see the whole animal. Peterson elaborates on that part of the elephant he knows best — Mormon country and the Southwest — which for him, constitute the West, but like one of the blind men, he senses that more of the thing exists.[3]

Specialization would seem to be one reason we have been unable to see the whole animal. Few of today's frontier scholars can claim the broad expertise of previous generations, perhaps best exemplified by Ray Allen Billington. In recent decades frontier scholarship has expanded at an exponential rate, and today's historian can only master complex though restricted areas under the broad aegis of frontier history — areas such as mining, women, urbanization, Indians, environment, agriculture, ethnic groups, politics, transportation, social relations, military affairs, and others. Researchers inside and outside academe who write on such topics often regard themselves as experts in narrow specialties and no longer identify with the broad field of western or frontier history. In truth there has been a sort of intellectual Balkanization* of western and frontier history taking place with few of us willing to acknowledge the process.[4]

It is my contention that an inability to define either the West or the frontier is at the heart of what some scholars have called the malaise of western history. Fortunately, intrepid individuals like Limerick and Worster are

---

*Balkanization. The act of breaking into smaller units and thus often undermining the whole. Specialization to the detriment of larger entities. The term arose from the controversial division of eastern Europe into several small countries, the Balkans. Those nations have often engaged in conflict.

willing to tackle the broad sweep of western/frontier studies. Yet critics of both the West as a distinct region and of the frontier process still seem to have the upper hand. Those who dispute regionalism declare the West to be a vast, divergent place that will not hold together as a unit. The extremes of geography, climate, ethnicity, and economy are well known, but the dissenters from regionalism postulate that forces of disunity are stronger. Subregions seem to fare better; the Great Plains, the Pacific Northwest, the Coast, the Rocky Mountain West, the Great Basin, and the Southwest coalesce well as distinct climatic and economic places. But how can a scholar unify an area containing Salt Lake City, Des Moines, and Los Angeles? Diversity is not the cement of regionalism.[5]

There is also a vagueness about the West's location. Where is it? Is Dallas in the West? Hawaii? What about those older places that were once the West like Illinois or Louisiana? Martin Ridge declares that "there is a psychological and not a physiographic fault line that separates regions." He adds, "there is a culturally defined public entity with geographic boundaries that is a part of the larger national whole to which it contributes and with which it interacts in a significant fashion." Ridge argues that what holds the West together as a distinct region is a shared series of "special experiences" which, when assembled, produce "a cultural basis for fixing boundaries of the West and for giving it meaning and significance. . . ."[6] But what are the cultural values and shared experiences that hold the region together?

If the West as a region is unfocused and vague, the definition of *frontier* is equally imprecise. When and where does the process commence and terminate? Do we use Walter Prescott Webb's "Great Frontier" thesis and start with Renaissance Europe? Many of Turner's and Webb's disciples believe that, above all else, the frontier was an economic evolution that explained American growth in the nineteenth and twentieth centuries. But within this Turnerian framework is an explicit rise-and-fall syndrome, a sort of nascent Marxism, that has caused more than a few frontier scholars, including Turner and Webb, to take a dim view of America's future. In contrast, Limerick looks back at a negative historical experience but seems to face the future with optimism, creating an almost perfect mirror image of Turner.

If the frontier has ended in the United States and the American economy entered into a twilight of decline, what has become of the capitalistic frontier? Logic dictates that it can be found in Singapore, Hong Kong, and South Korea. But this conception of the frontier as a synonym for *modernization* is so far-flung as to be almost meaningless. Scholars who subscribe to this view usually refer to a *developmental* thesis and avoid using the word "frontier." While this ethereal world frontier theory makes for heady reading, it falls to earth when confronted with the economic vitality of the Sun Belt since World War II. Decades ago, Turner's theories about democracy stemming from the frontier were attacked, and now many of his economic ideas seem equally outmoded. Assuming a close relationship between Marxist economic beliefs and the frontier thesis, the movement of socialist and communist countries away from Marxism bodes ill for the longevity of the traditional frontier process. The frontier thesis may well survive, but it will surely need significant rethinking.

The frontier can be seen, however, as a process, occasionally violent, which extended western civilization into the Far West. Limerick is correct in part that it was conquest, and Turner would agree. In his essay, "Pioneer Ideals and the State University," Turner wrote:

> The first ideal of the pioneer was that of conquest. It was his task to fight with nature for the chance to exist. . . . Vast forests blocked the way; mountainous ramparts interposed; desolate grass-clad prairies, barren oceans of rolling plains, arid deserts, and a fierce race of savages, all had to be met and defeated.[7]

But Turner's conception of the frontier can be distinguished from Limerick's in an analysis of the overall results that flowed from the conquest. Despite his concern for a frontierless America, Turner never doubted that something better followed for most individuals and the nation, and his contention would seem to have held true. Envision the possibility of California and the Southwest having remained a part of Mexico. The advantages to both conqueror and conquered would at least seem arguable. Do the millions of illegal aliens who have crossed the southern border in recent years come to live their lives as a conquered people? Without doubt, Native Americans suffered the most from the frontier process, but few Indians have been willing to abandon the material advantages of western culture. This was even true of earliest contact between Native Americans and Europeans when tribes possessed genuine independent existence. Furthermore, Native Americans have commenced the process of obtaining legal redress for cases of past victimization.

Capitalism, of course, arrived in the trappers' saddlebags and pioneers' wagons, but to argue that the West's economic history has been largely negative because of it flies in the face of the reality of our regional history. Moreover, the frontier was also legal, political, religious, philosophical, and artistic. Thus, a more modern usage of the word frontier carries far less economic connotation than it did for Turner, and comes closer to what others like Martin Ridge have called a cultural frontier — western civilization in all its varied aspects.

From the vantage point of 1990, the closing of the frontier is a far less distinct event than it was for Turner. Common sense indicates that as the

United States ages, the importance of the nineteenth-century frontier as a vehicle for self-definition will diminish. Still, most psychologists, like most historians of an earlier generation, recognize that formative experiences have a great impact upon the nature and character of the adult. As scholars, most of us have learned to cast a skeptical eye on autobiography, but we continue to think we can define ourselves with total objectivity. Less partial observers do a better job, and when one looks at how others define Americans, he or she finds that the American image abroad is drawn in large measure from the frontier. Tribal myths, the myths that create national character, are formed when nations undergo the creation process — they arrive early in the life of a people, a tribe, or a nation — and they last as long as the people themselves last, far beyond the actual conditions that create the mythology. There can be additions or subtractions, but national mythology remains constant at the core. Critics might rail that the frontier myth is dangerous and destructive, but based upon the history of other nations and cultures we would seem to be stuck with it. Like an unsavory relative, it's ours for better or worse.[8]

Unlike the frontier, the West as a region lacks an overreaching single historical or cultural experience that crystallizes its identity. Only two regions have such precision: the South, whose identity is delineated by slavery, secession, and defeat; and New England, whose identity is defined by Puritanism. One cannot find such common cultural underpinnings in the West. Instead, the West would seem composed of a series of overlapping characteristics that must be taken as a unit to fix the general location.

Many of the observations that follow are derived from my students at the University of Toledo, whom I ask, "What comes to mind when you think of the West?" The answers are written on the blackboard, and in about fifteen minutes we have an interesting definition, one that reflects the frontier image:

- *Cowboys.* What Donald Worster calls the pastoral West. Cowboys represent an on-going economic activity from earliest days that includes sheep raising.

- *Indians.* The living presence of Native Americans in significant numbers wtih an accompanying lifestyle that retains strong elements of traditional culture.

- *Aridity.* Particularly as defined by John Wesley Powell and Donald Worster. True deserts are only found in the American West.

- *Mountains.* Mountains that are geologically young. They have always been part of the public's image of the West, whether in the days of Thomas Jefferson, or John Muir, or 1990.

- *Hispanic influence.* Like Native Americans, the presence of Hispanic peoples in the West in significant numbers with a visible culture and influence.

- *Space.* Those parts of the West with fewer than six persons per square mile.

- *Mining.* The image of the mining West remains strong even though mining's importance in the region has declined in recent decades.

- *Federal government.* States with 50 percent of their land base controlled by government.

- *Long territorial experience.* States acquiring statehood after 1861 whose lengthy territorial experience was often colonial in nature.

- *Urbanization.* The West is the most urbanized part of the United States.

Students also often mention certain intangibles such as individualism, freedom, and violence, but I refrain from including these characteristics because they are subjective and cannot be mapped. Put each factor on an overlay, then put the overlays together, and you have one definition of the West. The edges lack convergence, but the process produces a western core, or "Heart of the West."[9]

Whatever inability we have in defining the frontier process or the region itself, however, there is no malaise in western history. When historians can engage in such fundamental debates over self-definition as we have witnessed in the last few years, one must conclude that extraordinary scholarly energy exists here. Consensus might well be an undesirable goal that is about as useful to historical creativity as a desert mirage. Moreover, western and frontier history, like the region itself, represent a big place with plenty of room for divergent opinions and multiple approaches to the subject. Recent discussion and argument are signs of intellectual vitality and should surely be encouraged.

A Longer, Grimmer, but More Interesting Story

BY ELLIOTT WEST

I have friends who say that a lot of the "new western history" is not really new, and that much of what is new is not really history. I disagree. It is true, I admit, that many new trends were anticipated by earlier writers. And certainly today's historians are borrowing from several disciplines, including anthropology, economics, psychology, environmental science, literature, and art.

Nonetheless, something new is definitely happening in the history business. The metaphors are tempting — our angles of vision are shifting, our embrace widening. However we describe it, the prevailing view of the western past has changed more in the last ten years than in the previous ninety.

This change is coming about through three lines of investigation. First, writers are reexamining the broad, overarching themes that explain western history. They have done so with two different goals in mind. Some have argued that it is time to stop thinking of the West as a place apart, a country with a setting and a story so different that it can be understood only on its own terms. Instead, say writers like William Robbins, our region's history should be seen as one result of developments that have transformed the nation and much of the world during the past few centuries.[1]

Many of these historians focus on one event in particular — the rise of a global capitalist economy. The dynamics and motives associated with capitalism can explain much about the West, past and present, from the restless and exploitive urges of pioneers, to the control and manipulation of resources by centers of corporate power, to the erratic, depression-prone economy of today.

Other writers have tried to bring together those themes that best explain the West's uniqueness. There are some obvious candidates, beginning with the weather. Western aridity tells us much about our development (and lack of it), our politics, and distribution of economic power. The West is different, others say, because of the extraordinary range of ethnic groups that have met (or rather collided) there. Still others point to the dominating presence of the federal government.

For all their differences, these theme-seekers have a couple of things in common. They play down, or deny altogether, the significance of the frontier, that European-American pioneering experience that has dominated almost utterly the earlier tellings of western history. Now the frontier is at most a chapter in a longer, more complex, and more interesting story.

Western history also feels different, for want of a better term, when told through these new themes. Under the older frontier interpretation, the story shimmered with a romantic, heroic glow. Suffering and tragedy were redeemed by the glorious results presumed to have followed — the nurture of American individualism and democracy and the coming of a civilized order into a wilderness. These new themes, by contrast, emphasize a continuing cultural dislocation, environmental calamity, economic exploitation, and individuals who either fail outright or run themselves crazy chasing unattainable goals.

A second line of investigation proceeds from the bottom up, taking a fresh look at particulars. It is a reconstruction of the basics: Just when does western history start? Who has shaped it and how? As a social historian with a nagging curiosity about how people have muddled through their days, I think the works in this second category are especially fascinating. They are also important, for, like the new themes, they challenge what have passed for generations as basic truths.

By the traditional view, for instance, western history basically begins with Lewis and Clark and ends with the Populists, and virtually everything in between is accomplished by adult males. Recent work is changing that perspective. Because of a prodigious outpouring of work on women's history, the story of settlement finally is going coed. Single women homesteaded, ranched, and ran businesses in the infant towns; wives played essential roles in their families' economic survival.

More fundamentally, these writers are telling us that we can best understand westward expansion not in terms of the bold and intrepid pioneer man but of his family (including, I should emphasize, his children). Families, it seems, were a key not only to economic transformations but also to social and even political changes, including the making of communities and development of labor unions.

Once we begin to retell part of the story, inevitably the rest begins to change. Women historians, for example, have shown how the first white fur trappers and traders relied on Indian wives, both as laborers and as essential liaisons in their first contacts with Native American societies. In time many of those Indian women were caught in the middle, without a place in either their original societies or the white communities then beginning to dominate the West.

Their dilemma in turn suggests another lesson taught over and over in the new history. Just as western expansion cannot be understood solely from the perspective of adult males, so the long-term story of the West is hopelessly distorted if we consider only the actions and interests of Anglo-American pioneers.

For one thing, the pioneer invaders were not all blue-eyed sons of Albion. Our region, in fact, was the most polyglot of the republic during those years. Recent issues of *Montana* have showcased the new work on ethnic history with articles on, among others, Irish, Chinese, Basques, French, South Slavs, Finns, and Nova Scotians.

More important, western history should be the history of everybody who has ever lived in the West. That sounds obvious, but in fact the story of many peoples has been told only in relation to the frontier epic of the last century. Reading older texts, for example, it is easy to get the impression that Indians and Hispanics were significant only as barriers to the bold frontiersmen who pushed beyond the Missouri after 1820. One wonders how the Nez Perce and Navajos survived the boredom of long centuries waiting for invaders from the East to show up.

The new history proposes that we think of the West instead as a land washed by successive waves of emigrants who have been moving, settling, and adapting to the country for at least twenty-five thousand years. The story does not stop with the homesteaders. Yet another wave, this one from the South, is rolling into the country today.

The nineteenth-century frontier was certainly one of the most important of those emigrant waves, but when we study it, we should include its full implications for those already there. Seen this way, the pioneer era was not all draped in glory. It brought a variety of disastrous changes. Consider, for instance, those familiar images of the pioneers: the plowman busting sod; bullwhackers driving their straining teams; cowboys watching over contented herds. These heroic portraits in fact depict an economic system that required a profound ecological transformation. These changes in the land left earlier inhabitants no alternative to new ways of living. Those lifeways in turn brought economic subjugation to their new military and political masters.

But there is more to the story than that. Indians and Hispanic natives may have been militarily subdued, but when we start to reconstruct the details, we find that, contrary to the usual "triumphalist" view, those cultures have been remarkably resilient. If much has been lost, much has survived, and there has been a vigorous exchange between the conquered and the conquerors, a cross-fertilization of customs, ideas, material culture, language, and worldviews.[2]

A dozen other examples could be offered, but these are enough to make the point. Reflecting the fresh themes of western history, the details of the story are being reconstructed.

There is a third perspective of the new history. As yet this line of investigation is rather unfocused, and it has drawn less attention than the first two. But it is full of promise. This perspective considers the emotional and psychological dimensions of western history, the human responses to the peculiar physical and social settings of the West. The other approaches consider western history from the top down and the bottom up. This one looks from the inside out.

The history of the West is partly that of perceptions. The same could be said of any region, of course, but given the new approaches to our story, human impressions take on an extraordinary significance. The West has been a place of very different peoples bumping into one another, of centuries of immigrants confronting the unexpected and trying to adjust to a demanding, changing environment.

Besides, people act according to how they see things around them. We cannot possibly grasp the Indians' resistance and accommodation, for instance, without some understanding of how they perceived the changes triggered by the coming of the Europeans. Nor can we explain the making of modern western institutions without some account of how their builders saw the country, its limitations, and their own roles and prerogatives.

As historians come to recognize the great diversity of the western historical experience, they have begun to reconstruct what its various peoples have seen and what they thought about what has happened. Ethnohistorians, for instance, are starting to answer some of western history's most intriguing questions: How did the Euro-American invasion appear to Native Americans, and how did their vision of the world change in response to those traumatic events?[3]

As for the pioneers, from their first glimpses of the West their impressions were far more diverse and complex than typically described. Women viewed the prospect of uprooting and resettlement with far greater trepidation than men. Men usually initiated the move west, but they, too, had their reasons for finding the change emotionally troubling. And the children, who were just learning to understand their surroundings, viewed the new land differently from adult men or women.[4]

Nowhere is this perceptual approach more helpful (and the older approach more worthless) than in charting the emergence of a modern regional identity. It is a commonplace that "the West is a state of mind." There is some truth behind the cliché; any region is, in part, what its people think about it. Westering settlers arrived with varied perceptions. During the years that followed the pioneers' arrival, many elements of western society engaged in a reckoning — natives with their new status; newcomers with the land's possibilities; everybody with ecological, social, and economic transformations as profound as any at any time in American history.

Making some sense out of this is one of the most formidable challenges to confront western historians today. Two recent books by Robert Athearn and Patricia Nelson Limerick have given us some cues.[5] In many ways these books could hardly be more different, but they have some things in common. Their historical terrain is that stretch of generations from the end of the last century until today. Between them they write of the persistence of old dreams of development and of recasting earlier, simpler myths into new forms. Most of all, they are concerned with what the West has meant to people, how those impressions have and have not changed, and how it all has made for westerners' sense of themselves and their place.

Several notable books have approached these same questions from other angles. To understand the modern West, we need to consider the region's literary and visual iconography. So some writers have studied the evolving images and impressions of the past century or more. Their sources have ranged from accounts of early explorers and travelers to the complex vision of contemporary novelists and artists.[6]

There is, in fact, a "new fiction" that has grown up alongside the new history. The novels and short fiction of Douglas Unger, James Welch, Patricia Henley, Craig Leslie, Kent Haruf, William Kittredge, Louise Erdrich, and David Quammen are stories of disappointment and persistence, grudging accommodations, the ghosts of traditions. Just as the new historians look hard at the romantic idealism of earlier works, these writers break with the easy heroism of the traditional western novel. There is little about promise but much about costs. Dreams have become obsessions and comic lusts. The characters — whether snake farm proprietors, rodeo Indians, or overmortgaged turkey farmers — are bound to the country by a bitter affection, a connection that is hard-earned and as inescapable as blood kinship.[7]

Novelists take liberties that historians are not allowed, of course. But these stories speak of emotional insights quite in line with recent historical works. They should remind us, I think, that the new history really is part of something larger. It is a maturing understanding of the West, a comprehension that takes into account the full length of its history, its severe limitations and continuing conflicts, its ambivalence, and its often bewildering diversity.

That still leaves room enough and more, of course, for other ways of looking at the western past. Certainly those who are fond of more familiar topics can still find plenty new to read. After all, two of the most successful books of the past few years have been Robert Utley's fine biographies of George Custer and Billy the Kid.

Notes for Thompson

1. Patricia Nelson Limerick, *The Legacy of Conquest: The Unbroken Past of the American West* (New York: W. W. Norton and Company, 1987), 17–32; Donald Worster, "New West, True West: Interpreting the Region's History," *Western Historical Quarterly*, 18 (April 1987), 141–56. [Worster's article appears on pp. 88–104 in this book.] For criticism of Limerick, see Donald Worster et al., *"Legacy of Conquest,* by Patricia Nelson Limerick: A Panel of Appraisal," *Western Historical Quarterly*, 20 (August 1989), 303–22; and Vernon Carstensen, "A New Perspective on the West? A Review of *The Legacy of Conquest,*" *Montana: The Magazine of Western History*, 38 (Spring 1988), 84–85. Worster's arid West definition is critiqued for narrowness by a number of scholars, including Martin Ridge, "The American West: From Frontier to Region," *New Mexico Historical Review*, 64 (April 1989), 138.

2. Gerald D. Nash, "Where's the West?" *The Historian*, 49 (November 1986), 1–9. See also Walter Nugent, "Western History: Stocktakings and New Crops," *Reviews in American History*, 13 (September 1985), 319–29; and Sandra L. Myres, "What Kind of Animal Be This?" *Western Historical Quarterly*, 20 (February 1989), 5–17.

3. Charles S. Peterson, "The Look of the Elephant: On Seeing Western History," *Montana: The Magazine of Western History*, 39 (Spring 1989), 69–73.

4. Roger L. Nichols, ed., *American Frontier and Western Issues: A Historiographical Review* (Westport, Conn.: Greenwood Press, 1986), 4–6.

5. Ibid., 1–2; Gerald Thompson, "Frontier West, Process or Place?" *Journal of the Southwest,* 29 (Winter 1987), 366–67.

6. Ridge, "Frontier to Region," 140.

7. Frederick Jackson Turner, *The Frontier in American History* (New York: Holt, Rinehart, and Winston, 1947), 269.

8. Ray Allen Billington, *Land of Savagery, Land of Promise: The European Image of the American Frontier in the Nineteenth Century* (New York: W. W. Norton and Company, 1981). Anthologies of world myths that include the United States draw the majority of American examples from the frontier and the West. Of course, see Henry Nash Smith, *Virgin Land: The American West as Symbol and Myth* (Cambridge, Mass.: Harvard University Press, 1950). See also American studies scholarly journals, such as *American Quarterly,* which contain countless articles on the ingredients of America's myths. Historians might well consider applying the techniques of Joseph W. Campbell to American mythology.

9. See Robert F. Berkhofer, Jr., "Space, Time, Culture and the New Frontier," *Agricultural History,* 38 (January 1964), 21–30.

Notes for West

1. William G. Robbins, "Western History: A Dialectic on the Modern Condition," *Western Historical Quarterly,* 20 (November 1989), 429–49.

2. For a few examples of books on these themes, see Richard White, *The Roots of Dependency: Subsistence, Environment, and Social Change Among the Choctaws, Pawnees, and Navajos* (Lincoln: University of Nebraska Press, 1983); Edward Spicer, *Cycles of Conquest: The Impact of Spain, Mexico, and the United States on the Indians of the Southwest, 1533–1960* (Tucson: University of Arizona Press, 1962); Sarah Deutsch, *No Separate Refuge: Culture, Class, and Gender on an Anglo-Hispanic Frontier in the American Southwest, 1880–1940* (New York: Oxford University Press, 1987); David Montejano, *Anglos and Mexicans in the Making of Texas, 1836–1986* (Austin: University of Texas Press, 1987); Albert L. Hurtado, *Indian Survival on the California Frontier* (New Haven: Yale University Press, 1988).

3. Elizabeth John, *Storms Brewed in Other Men's Worlds: The Confrontation of Indians, Spanish, and French in the Southwest, 1540–1795* (College Station: Texas A&M University Press, 1975); Penny Petrone, *First People, First Voices* (Toronto: University of Toronto Press, 1983); George Sabo III, "Reordering Their World: A Caddoan Ethnohistory," in George Sabo III and William M. Schneider, eds., *Visions and Revisions: Ethnohistorical Perspectives on Southern Cultures* (Athens: University of Georgia Press, 1989), 25–47. Work done on perceptions of Indians during the contact period of the eastern frontier suggests how useful this approach might be when applied to the Far West. See James Axtell, "Through Another Glass Darkly: Early Indian Views of Europeans," in *After Columbus: Essays in the Ethnohistory of Colonial America* (New York: Oxford University Press, 1988), 125–43; Mary Helms, *Ulysses' Sail: An Ethnographic Odyssey of Power, Knowledge, and Geographical Distance* (Princeton: Princeton University Press, 1988); James H. Merrell, *The Indians' New World: Catawbas and Their Neighbors From European Contact Through the Era of Removal* (Chapel Hill: University of

North Carolina Press, 1989); Christopher L. Miller and George R. Hamiell, "A New Perspective on Indian-White Contact: Cultural Symbols and Colonial Trade," *Journal of American History,* 73 (September 1986), 311–28.

4. Lillian Schlissel, *Women's Diaries of the Westward Journey* (New York: Schocken Books, 1982); Andrew J. Rotter, "'Matilda For Gods Sake Write': Women and Families on the Argonaut Mind," *California History,* 58 (Summer 1979), 128–41; Elliott West, *Growing Up with the Country: Childhood on the Far Western Frontier* (Albuquerque: University of New Mexico Press, 1989).

5. Robert G. Althearn, *The Mythic West in Twentieth-Century America* (Lawrence: University Press of Kansas, 1987); Patricia Nelson Limerick, *The Legacy of Conquest: The Unbroken Past of the American West* (New York: W. W. Norton and Company, 1987).

6. Patricia Nelson Limerick, *Desert Passages: Encounters with the American Deserts* (Albuquerque: University of New Mexico Press, 1985); Stephen Fender, *Plotting the Golden West: American Literature and the Rhetoric of the California Trail* (Cambridge: Cambridge University Press, 1981); Robert Thacker, *The Great Prairie Fact and the Literary Imagination* (Albuquerque: University of New Mexico Press, 1989); Howard Roberts Lamar, "Seeing More than Earth and Sky: The Rise of a Great Plains Aesthetic," *Great Plains Quarterly,* 9 (Spring 1989), 69–77; Becky Duvall Reese, *Texas Images and Visions* (Austin: University of Texas Press, 1983); Vera Norwood and Janice Monk, eds., *The Desert Is No Lady: Southwestern Landscapes in Women's Writing and Art* (New Haven: Yale University Press, 1987).

7. Douglas Unger, *Leaving the Land* (New York: Harper and Row, 1984); James Welch, *Winter in the Blood* (New York: Harper and Row, 1974); Patricia Henley, *Friday Night at Silver Star* (St. Paul: Graywolf Press, 1986); Craig Leslie, *Winterkill* (Boston: Houghton Mifflin Company, 1984); Kent Haruf, *The Tie That Binds* (New York: Penguin Books, 1986); William Kittredge, *We Are Not In This Together* (St. Paul: Graywolf Press, 1984); Louise Erdrich, *Love Medicine* (New York: Holt, Rinehart, and Winston, 1984); David Quammen, *Blood Line: Stories of Fathers and Sons* (St. Paul: Graywolf Press, 1988).

Making Connections

The questions that precede each selection are intended to help students see that essay in relation to the major question of this volume. But taken together, like an extended conversation, the essays also speak to one another. Sometimes the themes of the varied essays overlap and complement one another; on other occasions, authors and their ideas stand apart. The questions that follow should aid students in reexamining the larger query of the book while drawing ideas and interpretations from the entire collection: Does the frontier experience make America exceptional?

1. Can you summarize Turner's definition of the frontier and cite specific examples to illustrate that definition?

2. What segments of the frontier experience best exemplify the argument of America as an exceptionalist society?

3. Judging from the content of these essays and from what you know about the history of the United States, do you think the exceptionalist argument is valid? Why or why not?

4. White, Riley, Limerick, and West criticize Turner for not dealing with women and minority groups. Should a writer of the 1890s be judged by the expectations of the 1990s?

5. Several writers you have read, including White, Limerick, and Worster, call for a New Western history. How would you define this approach to the history of the American West? Do you agree with it?

6. Turner spoke of the frontier experience as a westward-moving *process,* but Limerick and Worster speak for the West as *place.* Which approach appeals more to you and why?

7. Ridge finds much in Turner's ideas still useful for understanding the modern United States and the American West. Do you agree with him? Which of Turner's arguments do you still find helpful?

8. Exceptionalism is a slippery and sometimes badly used concept. Should it be abandoned, or is it valuable in understanding American society and culture?

9. Which of these essays would you select as the most persuasive examination of the frontier/West, Turner, or exceptionalism? Why?

10. Can you think of any other interpretation of the frontier/West that is missing from these selections?

11. If you were asked to advance a hypothesis about the making of American society, would you argue for the frontier as the most exceptional force in shaping this identity? If not, what major influence has had a greater impact in your opinion?

Suggestions for Further Reading

For students wishing to read more about the frontier, Frederick Jackson Turner, and American exceptionalism, a large number of useful books and essays await them. These sources will help students expand their knowledge of these important and relevant subjects.

Several volumes provide general histories of the American frontier. The pioneering overview is Frederic Logan Paxson, *History of the American Frontier 1763–1893* (Boston: Houghton Mifflin, 1924). For an even more useful and thorough account, readers should consult Ray Allen Billington and Martin Ridge, *Westward Expansion: A History of the American Frontier,* 5th ed. (New York: Macmillan, 1982). Richard White provides the most up-to-date and the most interpretive treatment of the American West as an evolving region in his *"It's Your Misfortune and None of My Own": A New History of the American West* (Norman: University of Oklahoma Press, 1991). Less extensive but equally non-Turnerian in its emphases is Patricia Nelson Limerick, *Legacy of Conquest: The Unbroken Past of the American West* (New York: Norton, 1988).

Three books are particularly useful for additional information on Frederick Jackson Turner. The first of these, Ray Allen Billington's biography *Frederick Jackson Turner: Historian, Scholar, Teacher* (New York: Oxford University Press, 1973), remains the most extensive life story. It is thoroughly researched and well written. Meanwhile, Wilbur Jacobs discusses Turner as an important figure in the development of historical writing about the American frontier and West in his *On Turner's Trail: 100 Years of Writing Western History* (Lawrence: University Press of Kansas, 1994). Allan G. Bogue's *Frederick Jackson Turner: Strange Roads Going Down* (Norman: University of Oklahoma Press, 1998), the most recent biography, compares well with Billington's book. Exhaustively researched and balanced in its conclusions, Bogue's biography adds much new information about Turner as a teacher and a professional historian.

Although not all of Turner's writings are currently in print, several collections furnish selections from his most important work. Three of Turner's most important essays are gathered in Martin Ridge, ed., *History, Frontier, and Section: Three Essays by Frederick Jackson Turner* (Albuquerque: University of New Mexico Press, 1993). The same essays and several others by Turner appear in John Mack Faragher, ed., *Rereading Frederick Jackson Turner* (New York: Henry Holt and Company, 1994). All of Turner's most significant writings as well as the important books and essays written about Turner are listed in Vernon E. Mattson and William E. Marion, *Frederick Jackson Turner: A Reference Guide* (Boston: G. K. Hall, 1985).

Writings about American exceptionalism have proliferated in the past few years. For an instructive collection of essays about this topic, see Byron E. Shafer, ed., *Is America Different? A New Look at American Exceptionalism* (New York: Oxford University Press, 1991). Also consult Seymour Martin Lipset, *American Exceptionalism: A Double-Edged Sword* (New York: Norton, 1997). Especially helpful for understanding the relationship between the frontier and American exceptionalism is the provocative treatment in David W. Wrobel, *The End of American Exceptionalism: Frontier Anxiety from the Old West to the New Deal* (Lawrence: University Press of Kansas, 1993). In addition, three essays are illuminating on exceptionalism: Michael Kammen, "The Problem of American Exceptionalism: A Reconsideration," *American Quarterly* 45 (March 1993): 1–43; Ian Tyrell, "American Exceptionalism in an Age of International History," *American Historical Review* 96 (October 1991): 1031–67; and Martin Ridge, "Ray Allen Billington, Western History, and American Exceptionalism," *Pacific Historical Review* 56 (November 1987): 495–511.

Several other recent volumes trace shifting trends in historical writing about the frontier and American West. The most thorough of these is Gerald D. Nash, *Creating the West: Historical Interpretations 1890–1990* (Albuquerque: University of New Mexico Press, 1991). Essays on several notable western historians are collected in Richard W. Etulain, ed., *Writing Western History: Essays on Major Western Historians* (Albuquerque: University of New Mexico Press, 1991). Those wishing to sample the so-called New Western history should consult the writings of Richard White, Patricia Nelson Limerick, and Donald Worster in this collection as well as those mentioned in this list. Essays illustrating the New Western history as well as challenges to it also appear in Patricia Nelson Limerick et al., eds., *Trails: Toward a New Western History* (Lawrence: University Press of Kansas, 1991), and in Gene M. Gressley, ed., *Old West / New West: Quo Vadis?* (1994, Norman: University of Oklahoma Press, 1997).

Finally, two books by the editor of this volume deal with the changing interpretations of historians, novelists, artists, and movie makers in their works on the frontier and American West. See Richard W. Etulain, *Re-imagining the Modern American West: A Century of Fiction, History, and Art* (Tucson: University of Arizona Press, 1996), and Etulain, *Telling Western Stories: From Buffalo Bill to Larry McMurtry* (Albuquerque: University of New Mexico Press, 1999).